6-
2/7|
Essays

Looking Back

stories of our mothers & fathers in retrospect

Rebecca Wecks, editor

New Brighton Books

Credits

Li-Young Lee, "Furious Versions, Part 6" (excerpt) from *The City In Which I Love You*.
Copyright © 1990 by Li-Young Lee. Reprinted with the permission of BOA Editions,
Ltd.

Introduction excerpt from Blue Horses Rush In, by Luci Tapahonso. Copyright ©
1997 Luci Tapahonso. Reprinted by permission of the University of Arizona Press

For information on bulk purchases or group discounts for this and other New
Brighton Books titles, please contact us at 800-919-1779.
Visit our Web site: www.newbrightonbooks.com

Library of Congress Cataloging-in-Publication Data

Looking Back : stories of our mothers & fathers in retrospect / Rebecca Wecks, editor
  p. cm
  ISBN 0-9718377-4-0
1. Parent and child—Case Studies. 2. Parent and adult child—Case Studies.3.
  Mothers—Case studies. 4. Fathers—Case Studies. I. Wecks, Rebecca, 1951-

  HQ755.8.L665 2003
  306.874—dc22
                   2003049390

A Note from the Publisher

In two months my college-bound daughter will leave home and join her older brother in San Francisco. I have been trying to prepare for this milestone event when the roles and rules of parenting suddenly change. But it's hard to anticipate what emotional shifts will occur, and how they will play with my head and heart. Actually, I've been thinking more about how my son and daughter will look back on their childhood memories and I'm wondering how they would tell their stories in later retrospection.

Last year at this same time my thoughts were on my parents as I recollected memories of my own childhood. My mother had died quite suddenly a few months before, my father two years before her. The difficult job of working through grief brings unexpected opportunities for understanding, forgiveness, healing, and self-discovery. Said more simply, looking back often lets us move on.

Going back into my childhood memories I was struck with the realization that although the memories remained the same, what I could now understand about them had changed. New perceptions surfaced. A piece of information recently learned, or perhaps, just finally understood, now gave the memory a different meaning. This process of remembering my mother and my father brought me moments of connection, gratitude, inner peace, and longed-for love. Looking back did, indeed, allow me to move on.

And, so, this became the seed for *Looking Back: Stories of Our Mothers & Fathers in Retrospect.* I have been so pleased by the response to this anthology and have enjoyed the sharing of stories collected. They are as varied as human experience allows us all to be. But they also serve a common purpose—each story is written in honor of the father or mother who gave the writers the life experience to tell their story. These stories, therefore, are a tribute to all of them.

Finally, it is my hope that *Looking Back* will set you on your own journey of remembering. Perhaps the changes over time will bring you new understanding of your mother or father, and ultimately, of yourself.

—Karen Narita
June 2003

◄ ►

*In loving memory of
my father and mother,
George and Mary Narita*

◄ ►

Contents

Introduction

FURIOUS VERSIONS, PART 6

The night grows
miscellaneous in the sound of trees.

But I own a human story,
whose very telling
remarks loss.
The characters survive through the telling,
the teller survives
by his telling; by his voice
brinking silence does he survive.
But, no one
can tell without cease
our human
story, and so we
lose, lose.

Yet, behind the sound
of trees is another
sound. Sometimes, lying
awake, or standing
like this in the yard, I hear it. It

ties our human telling
to its course
by momentum, and ours
is merely part
of its unbroken
stream, the human
and other simultaneously
told. The past
doesn't fall away, the past
joins the greater
telling, and is.

—Li-Young Lee

Storytelling is older than language itself. From the beginning of time, people have been compelled to speak, write, paint, sculpt, or carve their stories as a legacy to be handed down from generation to generation. If we go back even further, prehistoric animals and plants, even the elements of nature have all left their stories imprinted on the face of the earth. Within the pages of this book are stories about mothers and fathers, all retold with a perspective that has broadened over time. Our life experiences reshape and color the lens with which we look on our past, and with time they evolve into stories rich with layers of meaning and potential.

Luci Tapahonso, in her collection of Navajo stories called *Blue Horses Rush In*, recorded a story entitled "White Bead Girl." In it the storyteller says:

One night my father was telling stories and he said suddenly, as if it had just occurred to him, "This thing called memory is like nothing else. Once you remember something, it never leaves you. It's how we know that we have lived."

Telling our stories can bring healing, understanding, and connection; and truly they confirm our existence. Telling a story about our parents can help us understand our relationship with them and, sometimes, why we are who we are. Each one of us can find someone to whom we can connect as we hear his or her story. In this way, listening to other people's stories can make us feel more connected to the rest of the human race.

The stories in this book are about the memory of a parent, and in the telling, the authors give us intimate information about themselves. Some of the stories are personal memories while others are fictionalized stories from the writer's experience. Each story, however, is told with a voice that has been uniquely shaped by the author's relationship with his or her parent. The stories are as varied as are the authors themselves. They range in content from positive, happy memories to those of disappointment and loss. While not all of them end in resolution, each author describes a shift in perspective realized by looking back and retelling his or her story. Collectively, these stories illustrate the extreme complexity and subtle nuance of parental relationships. The navigation through any relationship can be difficult, but there's probably not one of us who has not been mystified at some point by the profound affect our parents have on us, even as older adults.

As I was reading these stories, I found myself reflecting on my own childhood, growing up in a family of eight. A collage of images came to my mind of both my father and my mother. I wish to thank them for their participation in my life and for their love for me that seems to know no bounds. C. Marie Finn ended her story, *A Story of George*, (page 250) by telling her father, *"I am thinking of you now."* Mom and Dad, as I write this piece and look back on my life with you, I too am thinking of you now.

—Rebecca Wecks

The Second World War

RUTH NAYLOR

It was a Sunday in the 1940s. I stood at the foot of your bed listening to the heavy bass of your sobs, feeling the frame tremble like my heart. Our family had attended worship together as usual without you. You tried to join us for dinner; Mother had fixed your favorite— roasted chicken and mashed potatoes with a pool for gravy—but tears came to drown your appetite instead and send you back to a darkened room where my memory stands with you now that your life's battle is done. Your business buddy had been drafted. You couldn't see how to go on. Gladly you would have gone to the front instead, had you not been labeled 4-F. Poor vision was the problem. How I longed to scramble up onto the bed and hold you, comforting you with all the love I had to give. This was the first of only two times I'd ever seen you cry. Indeed, there was a war going on. One in the outside world you would have been glad to join and one inside your heart which you couldn't escape. I stood in awe at seeing my grown-up daddy cry, yet I was afraid to touch you who never held me close. I was afraid to ask you about the pain. I knew I'd only be in the way. "Don't bother Daddy," Mother said. "Come out and close the door." Headlines in the *Daily Times* blared stories of bombs, bayonets, and bloody beachheads. Mother's tears and our daddy's frequent absence led me to private lines in her diary. She should have known that inquiring minds could crack her code. A child knows. Children share their knowing. Cigarettes appeared in the glove box of your car. You didn't smoke. Then liquor that we Quakers didn't drink. But even those intended blows couldn't kill our mother's love for you. New images were more abusively direct. Lipstick on collars and handkerchiefs to twist the knife in her loyal heart. I forget who found the woman's panties in our car. One day we came home to find that you'd moved out! Your clothes were gone. Your closet empty. You'd live for now above your office. In one last ditch effort to lure you home, we made you a birthday cake, delivering it with your favorite chicken dinner. Your three spruced up children helped Mother deliver it to you and we watched as you took her in your arms and kissed her. Was that the only time I ever saw that? That was the second and last time ever (in more than 50 years) I saw you cry. Clearly the war was still raging inside. We grabbed a tiny balloon of hope and dreamed that you'd make it home. The battle that day was the last that Mother won. If you ever grew to feel victorious, it must have held little joy. I've never understood war—this or any other. So many casualties on home fronts around the world. So many weeping widows. So many orphans, maimed. While faulty eyes kept you from being drafted, you left wife and children wounded in your second world war. We still see clearly the bulletproof truth that all abhor.

The Road to Reconciliation

LAURA DAVIS

y mother and I are driving north to San Francisco. We've just passed the outskirts of Santa Cruz and the two-lane coastal highway opens up before us. I like road trips—the feeling of freedom and the sense of heading off on an adventure. For me, the car is a good place to talk; there's a unique feeling of privacy created in the front seat.

My mother has flown to California for an extended winter visit. She's been here two weeks so far. Although we've spent quite a bit of time together, we have never been alone. I have something I want to talk to her about, and I know this may be one of our few opportunities. So despite my nervousness, I plunge ahead. "You know, Mom, I'd really like to be closer to you, but sometimes when we're together and you start telling stories that go on and on, I feel further away from you. I feel more like an audience and less like we're in a conversation."

I hear a sharp inhalation beside me, then the sound of angry tears. These are familiar sounds; I know them well. Since my mother is a very emotional woman, I've never had to question how she feels. Now she is very upset.

"Oh no," I think to myself, "I never should have said that."

4

Temme lights into me, her words sharp and angry: "I was really looking forward to today because we haven't had a chance to talk, but you were just waiting to pounce on me, weren't you? I knew you didn't really want me to come on this trip today, and now you've sabotaged the whole day by starting it off with so much negativity..."

I feel my neck tighten and my body tense. An old sinking feeling starts at the base of my spine and moves straight toward my head, threatening to engulf me. I am sinking quickly and soon I will be nothing more than a puddle on the floor mat, sloshing remorsefully under the clutch.

I stop listening. I tune her out, a survival skill I mastered years ago. As numbness spreads through me, I keep my eyes fixed on the road, wishing I could feel something, anything. But there is no room for my feelings; Temme's are taking up every inch of space. I feel my mind snap shut and my heart harden. Pretty soon, there will be nothing left of me at all.

We're driving up Highway 1, the spectacular road that ribbons all the way from Mexico to Canada. I've had so many wonderful trips up this road—the elephant seals, the hang gliders, the surfers, the whitecaps—they're all streaking by as I sit locked in misery. I look out the window, wishing I could fly.

Then with conscious intent, I force my attention back into the car. I'm an adult, and I'm the one who instigated this mess; I'm the one who needs to clean it up.

Temme is still talking. I come in on the tail end of a speech I know by heart. "Why did you attack me like that? How could you be so insensitive?" As my mother's hurt spews out, I grow colder and more rational.

Like clockwork, our old patterns play themselves out. My mother pauses, then I know it's my turn. It's the old parry and thrust I know so well—she attacks and I defend. I attack and she defends. I respond automatically to my cue. "I wasn't trying to attack you," I say, my voice lofty and superior, "I was just trying to tell you something I thought might bring us closer together." I cringe as I hear myself defend my insensitivity. How arrogant and self-righteous I can be! All my mother needs is a compassionate word, a kind gesture, for me to reach over and take her hand, but something in me is frozen. I can't move.

She counters, "Well, it sure didn't feel that way to me." Lamely, I try to hold my ground. "No, really, Mom. I want to be close to you. That's why I told you it was great when you wanted to spend the winter here. It took a lot of courage for you to come here, and I admire you for it."

She responds, "I admit, you've been very generous. The maps you got for me, the kids' artwork in my room. You've invited me for dinner. You sent me all those news-papers with ideas of things to do. But underneath your niceness, there's always this formality, this coldness, this meanness just waiting to strike..."

"Mom, all I said is that when you tell a lot of stories, I

find myself tuning out. I don't feel connected to you and I want to feel more connected. That's why I said it. You have to admit it, Mom," I say, my voice softer now, "you do go on and on."

It's quiet on her side. The tears, I realize, are back. She's staring out the passenger window, lost in a private sea of pain. Finally she turns to me, her voice thick, "Do you have any idea," she says to me, each word deliberate, "what it's like to live alone? You have no idea! There is a hole in my life where family should be. Telling stories about places I've been and things I've done helps fill that loneliness. Why deny me that?"

My heart drops. I can't believe she's saying this about herself. Despite our history of estrangement, I've always admired my mother. "Mom," I say, "There are lots of great things about you. Look at what you've accomplished. Your husband walked out on you and you went to night school and got your master's degree. You pulled your life together financially. You've built a terrific network of friends. You have your theater and your health. You've traveled all over the world. There are a lot of good things in your life. Besides," I continue, "you don't have to be interesting for us. We like you just the way you are. You don't have to embellish yourself with stories."

My words don't penetrate. Her face is still anguished, her body pulled away. "You don't understand," she tells me, her voice wracked with pain. "You don't know what

7

it's like to be so far from my children and grandchildren. Everyone else has their family with them for holidays and birthdays, and I never have mine. You moved 3,000 miles away—and I know you did it to get away from me."

I say nothing. What she's accusing me of is true and we both know it. She goes on: "I don't blame you for that. What's done is done, but now you live here. You've made a life here—and I see that it's a good life. I accept that you're never going to move back to New Jersey. But I don't think you understand my situation at all. You're young. You're in the prime of your life. I'm past mine. My life is getting smaller and I'm alone. In my social circle, people are dying and a number of them are younger than me. I'm at the acceptable age for death and I've started to face my mortality. What's wrong with telling a few stories if they help me feel better?"

Wow. This wasn't what I intended. I didn't want to hurt her like this. I thought I was doing the right thing, but obviously I wasn't.

More than anything, I want to close up this wound and move back into the present, back into this glorious, sunny winter day. Then somehow miraculously we do. Neither of us wants to lose any of the ground we've so tenaciously carved out; we've fought for every inch and we're not going to let old history defeat us now. I push past my cold-ness and take hold of her hand. She pulls herself back from the precipice and we ease back into now. The terrible moment passes as we reach the Pigeon Point Lighthouse and continue north on 1 toward Half Moon Bay.

The rest of the drive, across Highway 92 and its rolling hills famous for pumpkin patches and Christmas tree farms then on to 280 North, a straight shot up to the City, we manage small talk—the kids, the garden, the fence Karyn and I are planning to build, the storytelling conference Temme recently attended.

But what I remember most about that drive north is that I finally understood that my mother was not my enemy, but rather a complex, imperfect aging woman too vulnerable to experience that conversation as anything other than an attack. Driving up to San Francisco, on that sunny winter morning, I realized with absolute clarity that any changes I needed to make in our relationship were going to have to happen inside of me.

Years ago, the question for me might have been, "Do I want this relationship? Is it worth it to me?" But that question had long since been answered. I was committed to her and she was committed to me. Now we were trying to figure out how to be two adult women together, and I realized that I cared enough about her to never want to repeat this scene again. The question I faced now was, "How can I find in myself the love, compassion, and acceptance for my mother that she so deeply deserves?"

Coastal Real Estate

DAVID GOGUEN

y mother wanted her ashes strewn into the ocean off a boardwalk in Ogunquit, Maine. I had agreed to this last act of kinship and carried out the request last August, two weeks after she had died. She never told me why the Ogunquit boardwalk was special to her, but I suspect it had something to do with romance. As I drove with her ashes down the road toward the ocean, an ambulance passed on the other side, and the sun flashing against its windshield burned white islands into the backs of my eyes. I looked at the urn of ashes sitting on the seat next to me. "Guess what, Mom?" I said aloud. "I own two islands in the back of my head—coastal real estate." Tears swelled and the islands wavered. Crying made sense. What good are islands without an ocean?

◀ ▶

She once whipped me with a red velvet rope I had stolen from the ticket line of a movie theater. I was fourteen years old at the time, and my mother said she'd teach me a lesson I'd never forget. The velvet rope didn't hurt as much as the metal hook at the end. When she finished, my back was black and blue from neck to waist. One of the blows had ripped a winding gash at an angle from my right shoulder blade to the hip. I still have the scar.

Debra asks me about the scar. In the three months that we've lived together, she's followed its path with her index finger, tracing its route over the bones of my shoulder blades to the smooth bow of my back. I haven't told her how it got there. I don't plan to tell her anything—at least until I can think of a story that's worthy of her. I tell each woman a different story.

◄►

My mother once told me that people who live on islands never have problems. They're lonely at first, she said, but they get stronger. When I was twelve, she woke me up one morning around three and told me to get dressed. I was still half asleep and asked what was wrong. She sat on the edge of the bed, and the weight on the mattress pulled me toward her. "We're going to the ocean," she said. "Hurry up and get dressed." I moved quickly, and moments later, I sat next to her in the car, driving through darkness. I fell asleep and when I awoke, we had crossed the New Hampshire border into Maine. The sun had just established itself in the sky.

Her hands were tight on the steering wheel, knuckles white. The muscles of her face quivered as if they had a life of their own. We ate breakfast at a McDonald's, where my mother bought a newspaper and opened the real estate section in front of her. Long after we had finished eating, she still sat there, circling ads. Her hands shook, and finally she left for the bathroom. I heard the static of water running behind the door. When she came out, her face was swollen and red. She looked at me and then at the newspaper spread out on the table. "I need a drink," she said.

◄ ►

Debra says the scar across my back looks like a dried riverbed. She laughs when she tells me this and begins singing. It's a song called "Horse with No Name," and she keeps singing one line over and over until I sing it to myself: "...And the story it told of a river that flowed made me sad to think it was dead." She has a beautiful voice, even though she's just fooling around. I can feel her finger following the scar, tracing its whiteness. She asks me again how I got it, but I'm not ready to tell her yet.

Maybe it happened during a thunderstorm—a bolt of lightning struck a power line, and a flailing wire branded the line across my back. Or perhaps I could say it happened while working on an Alaskan fishing boat one summer during college. I could tell her that two sailors pulled me into a room and tried to rape me, and when I pulled away, one of them strafed me across the back with a belt at close range. Or maybe I could use a minimalist approach. I could just say that a cable snapped—nothing more. I wouldn't offer any details.

◄ ►

The glasses my mother left in the sink always fascinated me on the mornings after her drinking binges. She would arrange them in a straight line, and I could tell which glasses she had used by the imprint of her lipstick on the rims.

They smelled like rotten fruit, filling the room with their sour odor. I found it odd that her glasses were always empty—coated with a dry haze that looked like the windows in the garage. The other glasses always had something left in them, usually a dull yellow liquid with a slight surface film. These glasses belonged to Jerry, my mother's boyfriend and the manager of the Village Twin Theater.

I knew Jerry mostly through the vinyl shaving kit he kept under the sink in our bathroom. He never paid much attention to me. I always sensed that I made him feel uncomfortable. Sometimes, I'd lock myself in the bathroom and put the toilet lid down, sitting with the shaving kit in my lap. The vinyl smelled like the bottle of after-shave inside. He had a bag of disposable razors in there, too, along with a toothbrush that had dried toothpaste on the stem.

Once, after Jerry had left for the theater, I poured some of his after-shave into my hands and slapped it onto the sides of my face. It was a Saturday morning after one of my mother's drinking binges. I went into my mother's room and stood in front of her near the bed. She stirred but never opened her eyes. Her nose twitched and she sniffed in my direction. "You're a sonofabitch, Jerry," she said, her eyes still closed. Then she reached for a glass on her nightstand, knocking a plastic alarm clock onto the floor. The clear face of the clock broke loose and rattled over the linoleum. I crushed it under the heel of my slipper on my way out of the room.

◄ ►

Debra says she can't understand my fascination with photographs. She stands on her toes in my darkroom and attempts to look over my shoulder at an image revealing itself in a developing tray. I lean forward to block her view. Under the safelight, I see the face of a homeless woman I had photographed a week before in a park. The features darken as the developing time expires and an alarm buzzes from the timer. Debra nudges me to the side. "Let me see," she says. As she steps forward, I turn on the light and the picture turns black. "Why did you do that?" Debra says, stepping back. I turn the light off and we stand in the red hue of the safelight. "I don't know," I say.

◄ ►

Jerry always came late to our house—after I had gone to bed. I'd hear him knock softly on the front door, followed by the wisps of my mother's slippers against the carpet in the hall. They'd pass my room and the shadows of their feet would stretch toward me in the light under the door.

They always whispered. Every now and then, I would hear one of them laugh. I always knew the exact moment the drinks were poured. The smell would find the cracks of my door and rise around me. I was afraid there would be an explosion. Fire. The odor of whiskey reminded me of an experiment in a science class, where a smoldering Popsicle stick was inserted into an oxygen-rich flask. It popped and burst into flames. They called it combustion.

◄ ►

I remember falling asleep on the couch late one day and awakening to the shrill cry of a smoke detector. The sound came from my mother's room, and when I had opened the door, the cigarette smoke was so thick, everything in the room had lost its color. She had gathered all of the ashtrays in the house and filled them with lit cigarettes. Smoke curled upward into a veil. I opened a window and swung a towel at the smoke detector until the noise stopped. My mother was lying on the bed, smiling at the ceiling, eyes rubbed pink like the meat of a salmon. She looked at me, but I felt transparent to her. I asked her if she was okay, but she had her own conversation in mind.

"I put the first one up for adoption," she said. "The second one went to heaven."

I asked again if she was okay.

"You were number three," she said.

I reached for her, but she pulled away. Her eyes turned back toward the ceiling.

"Jerry left me this morning," she said. "The sonofabitch left me."

She grabbed my arm and led me downstairs and out of the house. She opened the door of the car and pushed me inside. We drove fast down a long stretch of Euclid Street, weaving between the yellow center lines and a dark curb rising to the sidewalk. My mother opened the power windows with her master switch, and at once, the wind blew with such static that the smell of whiskey and her perfume was sucked past me into a stream of motion. My eyes made tears faster than the wind could take them away. Outside, the houses and their well-groomed lawns became a rainy window of color, each melting into one another.

"Mom!" I yelled over the wind.

Her foot pushed harder on the accelerator. We were pulled into a vacuum, and I felt as though I was being torn away from my seat belt and propelled into what had become of our lives. I saw our couch pitching end over end and kitchen knives and forks spinning in slow motion. A drawer of matched socks—still neatly folded—crashed into a cloud of chessmen and other game pieces. Did I scream at my mother again? Did I yell at her above the wind that hissed like old radiators in a church basement?

We parked in the lot behind the movie theater where Jerry worked. I followed my mother into a long ticket line that wound around the side of the building, shuffling forward until we came to a window. At that moment, my mother turned briefly to look at me. She bought us two tickets and we went inside. I didn't have time to think of what might happen next. We stood in the lobby amidst a crowd of people, until my mother caught a glimpse of Jerry moving near the concession stand. He was wearing a blue blazer with a gold nametag pinned over the right pocket.

"Hey!" my mother yelled.

Jerry didn't hear her over the low hum of voices.

"Hey!" she said again.

This time, Jerry saw her. He turned away and moved quickly in the other direction. My mother pushed her way through the crowd and yelled again. Jerry stopped and turned. The people in the lobby fell silent and opened a path between them. My mother stumbled forward, and I stood in her wake, smelling whiskey and perfume. She raised a finger toward Jerry.

"There's the actor," she said, addressing the people who surrounded her. "There's the fucking actor—look at him."

Jerry stepped forward to stop her, but hesitated.

"Look at him," my mother continued. "You want to see a good show? There's the greatest fucking actor who ever lived."

Nobody moved. My mother and Jerry stared at each other. Then, my mother swung a leg over a red velvet rope that stretched from the ticket line. She straddled the rope and began stroking it seductively.

"See this, Jerry baby? All my prayers have been answered. I don't need you anymore, do I?"

She moved her hips back and forth, rubbing herself against the rope. Two theater employees came and stood beside Jerry. "Take her outside," he said. They responded immediately, each taking their place beside my mother. They grabbed her arms and pulled her through the crowd toward the door. I started to follow them, but stopped to look back at Jerry. He had taken a few steps back. Our eyes locked.

"Leave me the hell alone," my mother yelled at the theater employees. She flailed her legs and arms.

I turned and ran after my mother, following her outside onto the sidewalk. She moved quickly and disappeared around the side of the building. By the time I had reached the parking lot, she drove past me in her car, not even noticing that I was standing there. For almost an hour, I sat next to a navy blue dumpster, waiting for her to return, but she never did.

When I realized she wasn't coming back, I walked around to the front of the theater and cupped my hands against the dark-tinted window to look inside. The lobby was empty, except for three teenagers who were laughing and throwing popcorn at each other at the concession stand. I stared at the red velvet rope near the ticket line. I don't remember the exact moment I went inside and stole the rope. The entire act was blurred, like I was back speeding in my mother's car with the windows open and my face stung by some invisible current.

◄ ►

Debra says she can't wait anymore. "You know what I'm talking about," she says. I open my mouth to speak, but she takes my hand and puts a finger to my lips. "Don't say anything," she says, and I obey. We sit in silence and I hear things I've never heard before, like heating vents clicking in the walls and the breeze outside making an antenna wire flap in the eaves of the house. I feel a deep loneliness rising in my head, and when I finally speak, I tell her that my mother once whipped me with a red velvet theater rope. Debra's expression doesn't change. It's just another story to her. One of many.

◄ ►

Before Debra left me, I had photographed her in an abandoned house we found on a dirt road near Machiasport, Maine. Her back was to the camera, and she stood in an open doorway, staring out into the light. On each side of the door were two window holes. Broken glass made jagged mountains rise from the sides of each pane. Later, when I printed the photograph, I noticed how light from the door and windows had formed a cross around her. It was like she was crucified in that old house. Behind her was a broken floor littered with splintered wood. Strips of ceiling curled down from above. Debra always found it odd how I would sit for hours and stare at that photograph. Even now, when I hold it in front of me, what can I say about the woman in the picture, except that she hangs in the light much in the same way my mother did when her ashes hit the air in Ogunquit, Maine? It was a moment of wealth. We both owned something then.

My Mother Through a Window, Smiling

CHERIE JONES

t he fallen branches of every tree I have watched grow for the first eighteen years of my life die at my feet as I walk my baby home. My mother is visible through the door to the front room. She is sitting at the kitchen table, which, today being wash day, is naked. She has already scrubbed it with bleach and stripped the wood of color and texture. It is dull, pale, and clean. She is hunched over, elbows on the table, breathing fire into the telephone. Her large legs are spread and her feet are flat on the floor. They are archless, swollen feet—no more than usual—and the cracks of her heels yawn when she shifts her weight from one leg to the other. Her feet are stained by dust. They are so large and grip the ground so firmly that it is hard to imagine her ever having been swept off them. But then she has never claimed to have ever been swept off them. She has never admitted to having done anything so frivolous as fall in love.

My mother is eating the assorted leftovers of the past few days: black pudding stuffed into the taut tyres of pig intestines; fried flying fish; breadfruit; pickled cucumbers.

She herself will say that she hates breadfruit but she will also say that food must not be wasted. The heads of the fish have been forced open to let the tails come through their mouths like the mocking tongues of cruel children. Their spines have been broken to facilitate the bending, and my mother, content, is crunching bone and spitting what cannot be swallowed onto a piece of newspaper in front of her in between words. I imagine her saying "for the cat."

Through the doorway my mother is remonstrating into the telephone receiver, propped into the fleshy curve of her neck. She keeps glancing at a clock ticking in the belly of Jesus above the kitchen sink. She is wondering whether I will come back after all, or whether she will have to credit me with being a woman of my word. She looks outside and nods knowingly. When she comes to the doorway she refers to the last thing I said when I called to say I was pregnant and we argued. She says, "Well, I see you are not dead."

"No, I am not dead," I say.

Against my better judgment I am decidedly alive. She takes the baby and turns her back to say her good-byes. I step over the threshold as he coos at her, unwary. I go in and close the door. The crook of my arm cools quickly.

"She is here," she says to the telephone before replacing it. She sets a place at the table and to my baby she says, "Come and meet your grandfather."

She goes out the back door which, when opened, lets

21

in the whistle of a machete on greenery. It is the time for the trees at the back of the house to die. I sit on a chair. It is hard and familiar.

"How was your flight?" my father asks when he comes in. He sits behind a plate of hot pudding and cold lemonade that she sets before him. In his glass the ice melts a little and sinks lower in silence. My mother returns to her bones. The baby cries.

"It was alright," I say. "Long."

She pauses from her grinding, "Here," she says, "or he will think he is mine."

When I take my baby he starts to wail. I try to nurse him but he rejects my breast, looking at me in bewilderment. I am already a stranger.

"He is not hungry," she says, her eyes still on her bones, "he is probably sleepy."

"He has not eaten since we left Heathrow," I dissent, but my voice is weak, plaintive. "He must be hungry—he slept all through the flight."

I am rubbing my nipple across his lips. He is turning his head and screaming. My father averts his eyes.

My mother chews her last fish head thoughtfully and the eyes disappear with two wet slurps of her lips and a sigh. Even with evidence of my womanhood she fears she cannot attribute to me certain womanly talents. She takes the newspaper to the back door and spreads it at her feet. She calls the cat who waits for her to retreat before he approaches his dinner. She washes her hands slowly, dries them, and returns to me on her solid feet. She does everything noisily, and between her and the baby I am almost beside myself. When she takes him I am relieved.

"Come to mama," she says to my son, "you poor, sleepy baby."

She starts to sing a nonsense song:
Big Rat had a spree
L'il Rat went to see
Big Rat take up L'il Rat
and throw him in the sea...

My mother says "Big Rat" like it is someone she knows. It could be a neighbor or a friend. It could even be herself. But no image presents itself for "L'il Rat." My son's eyes start to close and his wiggling stills with her patting. It is her manner more than her method that he responds to. She is the woman of this house. When I became as infantile as he is he did not know me.

"You are looking like your Aunty Sissy," she says to me in the new silence, "Dads, don't she favor Sissy?"

My father scrutinizes my face like he would a picture of a remote relative.

"A little," he says.

My mother smirks.

"But Sissy run to fat. She don't work as hard as I do. All she do is have babies for foolish men."

She looks hard at me.

"What is it you were studying again, before this?"

"Voice, I was training my voice to be a singer."

It had been a bone of contention in its day—before it became negligible in the face of an illegitimate baby. Who in their right mind traveled thousands of miles and borrowed money to learn how to sing? Singing was not something that people needed. You could not eat it, wear it, or use it to survive. Who studies something that you either can or cannot do? Only someone idiot enough to turn around and spoil it all by having a baby without the security of a husband.

"Your song is probably too sweet," says my mother.

"Some girls cannot tell the difference between a man who wants to help her sing a song and a man who just wants to hear it," says my father.

"Finish your food," says my mother.

My father gulps the last of his lemonade, the ice so small he swallows it all with one quiet motion. It makes no sound on its way into his throat. And he returns to the murder of the garden.

My mother tells me that he started to axe the trees since I called and told them I was taking a year off college to come home with the baby. It has been three days and they are almost all gone. The mammy-apple, the breadfruit, the cherry will henceforth be referred to in the past tense. She starts to sing a hymn. A requiem for the departed.

She is removing my father's setting with one hand and

holding my baby with the other. She has rendered me useless and I take as long as I can to replace my breast.

"Your old friend Mellie has gone to Cuba," she informs, "on scholarship to study Doctor-work."

Loosely translated it would read something like, "Mellie is making something of her life and learning something people can use."

We are momentarily lost in our private thoughts. When we speak again, it is at the same time.

"She will probably come back home soon with a Cuban baby."

"That's good. Mellie's very bright."

"What?" she asks, with her eyes flashing.

My father's Pyrex bowl has fallen but is not shattered. The noise starts the baby crying again.

"About the scholarship," I say.

I take my baby from her arms and put him over my shoulder. She eyes my hold on him with doubt. I pat him and he burps and then he settles down again. When he does she sucks her teeth as if she has already forgotten about Mellie. She is singing her hymn again. It may be for herself.

"Come," she says to us, quietly, "let me show you where to put him down."

She goes up the stairs on her solid feet, the cracks of her ankles yawn with each step.

Full Circle

MITALI PERKINS

he electricity was out, and David had disconnected the noisy generator. Candles in clay pots threw circles of flickering light across the screened verandah. Warm winds danced through the coconut trees and brought the heady smell of jasmine, the promise of rain. A Bangla song drifted over the high gate.

Ruma tilted her head forward, hoping that David would find that place on her right shoulder that never relaxed. She could feel it even after two sets of singles at the Embassy club and a luxurious bath. His fingers probed, found the tightness, began to battle it. Ruma exhaled slowly so he wouldn't notice her relief.

"I have a going away present for you," David said.

"I don't like presents, remember?"

"You'll like this. I'm visiting a project in Faridpur tomorrow. And you're coming along."

She whirled around to face him. "David! Really? Are you sure it's okay?"

"I cleared extra hours for the jeep and driver. Visiting an ancestral village qualifies as cultural orientation. It would help to know the name of it, though."

"Poshora." She said it quickly, surely, with the

"shaw" sound that was difficult for foreigners. "Pasera," they would say, if their cleft palate and ear hadn't formed around Bangla. "I can already imagine my dad's reaction to this. His daughter visiting the so-called 'shoythan Muslim family who stole our land.' Isn't it interesting how the Bangla word for evil sounds like Satan?"

David settled the pillows behind her and began working on her left shoulder. "Your grandfather was a land-owner, wasn't he?"

"And his grandfather before him. They owned a jute farm and exploited their Muslim workers."

"You do have to be careful, Ruma. I've heard of Hindus trying to re-claim land lost at partition. They say that Muslims are angry because the courts are giving land back to Hindus."

"Too late for my grandfather," Ruma said. "He tried hard, though. He must have sent fifty letters full of legal threats from Calcutta."

"When did he finally give up?"

"He didn't. He ignored his children, chewed betel leaves, and died a bitter old man. You know how Dad's been affected. He never really settled in America. He talks about Poshora like it's some kind of lost paradise."

"I'm a little worried about this visit," David said. "Whoever lives there now is not going to be happy to see you."

Ruma was quiet. Then she said: "I'd like to make it clear that we don't want the property back. End this bitterness once and for all."

"How're you going to do that?"

"Easily. Drive up in a big American embassy vehicle with a big white guy. Shower their children with gifts. Wear my fanciest clothes."

"Speaking of clothes, I still can't get used to seeing this on you," David said, fingering the soft silk of the scarf draped over her shoulder. She was wearing a sky blue *salwar chameez*, which was a matching set of baggy pants, long tunic, and scarf.

In Calcutta, where she'd stayed for a week before coming to Bangladesh, Ruma had waited in vain by the baggage claim. She'd exited the terminal with only her carry-on and traveling clothes. Delighted over their American niece's first visit in a decade, her aunts and uncles showered her with Indian replacements. She'd stepped off the plane in Dhaka wearing a green silk sari, golden bangles, and high-heeled sandals, and David had pretended to collapse. He was used to her graduate school clothes—cotton pants, baggy sweaters, and loafers.

A dry cough sounded in the doorway. It was Masjid, David's valet, fluent in Victorian English, who referred to himself only as "Bearer."

"Excuse me, sir. Would you kindly oblige by indicating whether Bearer should calendar your navy trousers?"

"No, thank you," David replied. "I'll wear the brown ones."

"As you wish, sir. I shall take my leave." Bowing stiffly, without a glance at Ruma, he disappeared.

Once again, he had flung disapproval over Ruma like a heavy veil. Masjid was a master of the Bengali art of silent communication. Even the smallest Bengali child could raise an eyebrow, wrinkle a nose, lift a chin. Ruma's immigrant parents had not managed to pass on any of this elaborate system of gestures. Now she wondered if this was why she'd become fluent in five languages, accumulating words to offset the loss of body language.

Masjid's interruption had ended their conversation, and David joined her on the sofa. They often sat together like this, diplomat and linguist, abandoning their tools of trade and sinking into comfortable silence.

A gust of wind blew out one of the hurricane lamps, and the monsoon rain began to drum overhead. Before she could anticipate the change in his mood, David reached over to pull Ruma close.

"Marry me, Ruma," he whispered, under the percussion of the rain.

Ruma let herself rest against him for a moment before pulling out of his arms. Then she stood up. Retreating, she avoided his eyes, and made herself stop at the doorway.

"We'll probably leave early tomorrow—I'm going to my room," she said, hating the low, unsteady candles for making David seem even more alone on the sofa. She turned and left the verandah before he disappeared entirely in the darkness behind her.

◄ ►

The ferry pushed steadily through the currents of the Padma River. Mid-morning sunshine spangled the water. Fishermen called greetings from rafts to sailing boats, and huge, silvery fish leaped unexpectedly into the air. Passengers perched precariously on the open edges of the ferry, sipping tea from tiny china cups. They watched as Ruma and David squeezed through lines of parked vehicles.

At the tea-seller's stall, Ruma leaned against a barrel and clutched her cup of tea.

David broke the silence. "Sorry about last night," he said. "Temporary insanity. First-term culture shock."

Ruma took a big gulp of hot tea. "It was my fault," she answered. "I don't want to hurt you, David. I shouldn't have come."

They were quiet again. Then he nudged her, and pointed to a low country boat passing by. "We both needed a rest," David said. "That's why you came."

Inside the boat, five sand-haulers lay beside their empty buckets on a flat bed of sand, fast asleep. They were leaning against each other in an intimate tangle of cigarette smoke, brown limbs, and plaid *lungees*. Ruma watched them until they disappeared.

In Faridpur, Ruma asked David to drop her off at the

market while he did his work. She wandered through the stalls, enjoying the easy give and take of bargaining in Bangla. A blue sari with delicate white embroidery caught her eye, and she bought it, along with sweets, trinkets, and toys. She tucked 100 *Taka* notes, worth about three dollars each, into separate envelopes.

It was almost two when the car arrived. David handed her a turmeric-stained cardboard container of chicken curry, and Ruma watched the passing countryside as she ate. Spiky clumps poked out of muddy rice paddies, fed by slim chains of water. Hibiscus bushes leaned over ponds of floating purple flowers, like dancers trying to see their own reflections.

The driver stopped for directions, and they climbed out into the heavy, still air of mid-afternoon. Purple and blue cotton saris were slung across the open windows of a clay house. A breeze lifted the light material, and Ruma glimpsed three babies sleeping side by side on a bamboo cot.

An elderly man stood by the door, smiling toothlessly. He was wearing a white *dhoti* instead of a lungee, which marked him as one of the few remaining Hindus in Poshora. "Banerjee house?" he repeated. "Yes, yes. It's still standing. Last house down that lane, about three kilometers, just past the bridge." He peered up at Ruma through thick lenses. "So you've come back, have you? High time. That son of a scoundrel will be more than surprised to see the face of a Banerjee again."

Ruma nodded, too surprised to answer.

"You've still got the Banerjee face," David said, as the jeep hurtled over the narrow, muddy road. "This could be more dangerous than I thought."

Ruma handed her camera to David. "Not once he understands why I'm coming. Take photos for Dad, will you?"

They rattled over the bridge, and the driver turned off the engine. "Banerjee house," he announced, like a conductor at the end of the line.

Ruma's eyes quickly scanned the property. A square bungalow, paint peeling, faded green shutters closed against the afternoon sunshine. Two huge mango trees, laden with fruit, shading a wide, grassy space in front. A dirt path winding down to a pond, lined with purple and white bougainvillea. Tops of countless fruit trees in a grove behind the house. Beyond, a sea of jute, with no other house in sight.

She walked to the threshold of the house, with David snapping photos as he followed. Before they could knock, a man came out, re-tying his lungee. He shut the door firmly behind him, but Ruma could see a row of eyes peering through the slats of the window shutters.

"What do you want?" the man demanded, his glance shifting back and forth to settle on David's face. "I have no business that concerns any Americans."

David stepped back, and raised the hand that wasn't

holding the camera. "It is not my business," he said in simple Bangla.

"What does she want, then?" the man asked.

Ruma held out the bag of presents. "I am Dilip Kumar Banerjee's granddaughter. I came with gifts for your children before departing for my home in America."

The man was quiet; his eyes now focused on Ruma, measuring the unspoken language that would either vindicate or contradict her claim. Ruma held his gaze, keeping her whole body still.

Suddenly, the man clapped his hands twice. "Bring tea!" he shouted. Ruma heard muffled gasps come from inside the house and then a scurrying began. Pots and pans clattered and a baby began to wail.

The man led them to a shady bench. "You speak Bangla well," he said to David. "What is your job?"

As David stumbled through his language school answers, Ruma finished her tea. She could hear laughter, conversation, a creaking pump handle in the distance.

"May I go inside?" she asked, standing up.

The man nodded. "Your husband will remain with me." David winked at her behind the man's back.

Ruma gathered up the presents and walked to the house. Once again, the door opened before she could knock. A tide of women and girls engulfed her and pulled her inside. Curious hands smoothed the material of her salwar chameez, fingered her bracelets, and caressed the skin of her forearms. A flood of questions in village Bangla swirled around her. Quickly, a young girl pulled a chair under a fan and wiped it clean with a damp cloth. Two of the oldest women seated Ruma, like ancient handmaidens attending a foreign queen.

Ruma counted thirty-five female faces beaming at her in a semi-circle. Shy children peered out from behind their mothers' saris.

"Come," Ruma said, reaching into her bag. She spread out the toys and sweets, and the children came, their eyes bright. Ruma began tucking envelopes into their shirts while their mothers tried to stop her.

"You should not give this kindness to us," one of them protested.

"It is my privilege," Ruma answered. "Where is your new bride?"

The girl who had polished the chair was pushed forward. "She has married our third son," the oldest woman said.

Ruma handed her the blue and white sari. The girl lightly traced one loop of the embroidery, grinned at Ruma, and slipped away.

A baby tried to climb on Ruma's lap, his naked body camouflaged in talcum powder. He tugged at her leg, frowning, demanding. In English, softly, Ruma told him: "It's yours, baby. Yours to keep. We don't want it back."

The baby was whisked away to make room for another

cup of tea and biscuits. When Ruma finally stood to go, a chorus of protests arose again. The circle of women, their hands constantly caressing, clustered around her as she made her way to the door. She turned for one last look, one last smile, before stepping into the empty courtyard. The door closed behind her.

She wandered down to the pond, recognizing landmarks from stories her father had told. Stooping, she splashed water over her hot cheeks, drying them on her scarf. She gazed across the water, knowing that in places it was too deep to measure. *Here my great-uncle drowned when he was three.* Turning, she climbed the steps and walked behind the house, touching the clay walls that housed chickens in cool, connected holes. *Here my father ran his hand along the length of a sleeping python as he hunted for morning eggs.* She counted fruit trees: thirty-two banana trees, seven guava trees, fourteen mango trees, countless coconut and lychee trees. *Here, in the great storm of 1936, lightning destroyed the tallest mango tree in Poshora.*

Jute fields stretched out to the horizon, thirsty for rain. Sitting on the stump of the dead tree, Ruma imagined the woman she might have become—a matron in an arranged marriage, dutifully bringing her children from her husband's home to visit Poshora.

Be thankful for freedom, the American dream, that independence you guard so fiercely, she told herself, trying to silence the raucous chorus of guilt, desire, and fear inside her head. These were familiar enemies, hurling their accusations each time she pushed David away. But now a new voice joined their clamor—the sharp staccato of envy. Envy of the woman she might have been. Envy barking out the list of Ruma's losses: a community of decision-makers; the tutoring of tradition; predictable rites of passage; a circle of connection. Gone, gone, all gone, with nothing new to replace them.

When she finally headed back to the bench, black crows rose from the trees, flying west against a fading sky, calling to one another. David stood up to meet Ruma, and so did the man.

"Ready to go?" David asked. He sounded eager.

Ruma turned to the Bengali man. "Do you have any old letters or papers that belonged to my family? I'd like to give them to my father."

The man frowned. "We kept a trunk of some such things. Photographs, letters, school certificates. But nobody came for them."

"May I have them?" Ruma asked. He hesitated. "My father took care of them," he said.

Ruma came forward, caught and held the man's eyes. "What did he do with them?" she asked. The answer came in a low voice. "He burned them." Nobody spoke.

"I am sorry for that," he said finally, ending the silence.

Ruma stepped back then, and nodded. Their eyes met in one more unspoken exchange. Then she walked to the mango tree, leaving David to complete the elaborate courtesies of farewell. She plucked one yellow-green mango and held it in her palm. The fruit glimmered in the last light like a huge opal. Ruma peeled the skin back and took a bite.

"Are they ripe?" David asked, coming to stand beside her.

Ruma hurled the rest of the mango as far as she could. It landed with a distant, muted splash in the pond. "Not yet," she answered.

Turning to face him, she gathered up his hands, one in each of hers, like one shy child inviting another to join a circle game.

The Stars Are Ours

TOM SKIERKA

All I need is a broken-in Lazy Boy and the stars to steer her by.

I am the captain of this starship, an old brown recliner left over from our neighborhood garage sale. Right now, however, it appears to be the best investment I ever made. I anxiously await every flight and will not relinquish command of the bridge for quite some time.

My navigator climbs aboard the bridge, which doubles as my lap. She is my two-year-old daughter Olivia, who knows these stars better than anyone in the galaxy. She should. She named every one of them. She introduces them to me, pointing, "That's the Mommy star. There's the Olivia star, and there is the Daddy star."

"The moon?"

"That's home."

The night sometimes gets chilly, requiring an extra blanket or two. While waiting for a falling star to wish upon, I softly sing her my favorite songs until she falls asleep. I pick her up, carry her to her room and tuck her in, then return to the night voyager and watch the rest of the late show. Kicking back in the chair, I fly solo into memories I logged by these stars.

Shortly after Olivia's birth, my wife Tanja and I spread out an old blanket in the backyard and put her between us. Olivia would giggle and reach for those twinkling lights. As she got older, it became a bedtime ritual that was only occasionally hindered by seasonal changes and unpredictable weather. At these times she would look at the snow or the falling rain and sadly say, "No stars tonight." For her second birthday, I found tiny glow-in-the-dark stars and moon stickers in a toy store and created a constellation in her room. At bedtime, I turned out her light. She let out a happy sigh and asked, "Are those stars ours?"

I kissed her cheek, and told her they were hers to keep. She hugged and thanked me, then started naming them. I looked at our private universe on her ceiling. They reminded me of my father and the nights he and I shared, many similar to the ones I was spending with Olivia.

I found myself drifting back to my childhood camping days at Priest Lake, Idaho. Dad and I spent many nights playing cribbage or casino by lantern light while looking for a baseball game on the radio. We'd place little bets on the Spokane Indians game, with me rooting against the home team, since they were future Dodgers and I was a die-hard Giants fan. After the game, we'd blow out the lantern and then throw water on the fire. We watched the steam rise and disappear into the night sky and declare that we were creating tomorrow's clouds. We'd put on flip-flop sandals he bought at the bait store and walk along the beach telling old jokes oft told but still making us laugh. Dad reminisced about how he and Grandpa used to stay up late and watch the stars from the porch in Brewster, Washington, listening to baseball on the radio. Looking at the majestic sparkles, and the occasional flare darting across the sky, we tried not to stumble into the lake for an unexpected midnight swim.

Awakened by those memories and the splashing of the automatic sprinkler system, I dashed back into the house and passed by Olivia's room. She was clutching her *Good Night Moon* book. I turned off her night lamp and looked at her luminous ceiling and thought about those nights and that Milky Way at Priest Lake. I could hear Dad's stories and feel the wet sand on my feet. I could smell the campfire and see the moon reflecting off the water. It was something I couldn't buy and stick on a ceiling. I heard a murmur and turned. Smiling to myself, I decided to return to Priest Lake and give Olivia those stars.

We arrived just before the sun set. Tanja had to work and wouldn't be able to join us until the next day. Olivia was excited about our first camping trip together. After setting up the tent and camp, it was getting dark and the night sky called. I grabbed a blanket, put Olivia on my shoulders, and walked down to the beach. Her little hand cupped under my chin steering me clear of rocks and

trees. The sand, still warm from the afternoon swelter, was comfortable to sit on as we watched the sun drop into the lake. It had been so hot I couldn't blame it. The moon rose from the water and signaled the stars to appear. It reflected off the lake in full illumination. Olivia recognized most of the stars, and was amazed that they had so many friends she had never seen in the city. I told her about the shapes, the constellations, and where some of the planets were. Suddenly her excited little voice became silent and then sad.

"What's wrong honey?" I asked.

She pointed to the moon and said, "Home. Mama's there. Good night Mama."

Olivia and I sat, admiring the brilliance of the sights and sounds of the night. I sang to her softly until I felt her little head rest on my shoulder and her breathing become deep. Cradling her, I walked back to camp, placed her in her sleeping bag, and returned to the campfire. I looked for a baseball game on the radio. No luck. I turned it off and then I, too, looked up at the moon and said "good night" to Tanja.

Dad stayed up late after all us kids went to bed. A few times I tried to sneak back out, but I had no stealth when it came to unzipping a tent. I could hear him, talking to the stars. "Good night Mom and Dad," I heard him say one time. I wasn't sure what that meant at the time.

Olivia woke shortly before sunrise and decided it was time for us to get Mommy before the stars went away. Knowing it would be impossible for her to go back to sleep and knowing that my fellow campers wouldn't want to hear an extremely tired Daddy trying to reason with a very upset two-year-old about why we couldn't share her new found discovery with her mommy, I decided to let our adventure start very early that day. We left our campsite to pick her up from work. On the way home that dark and sleepless morning, Olivia looked out the window and said, "Daddy look! The stars are coming with us and so is the moon!" then she fell back to sleep.

I guess I know why Dad never got much sleep on those trips and why he laughed when I told him it was a great way to relax. I drove in silence, softly singing. She slept in her corner, dreaming of bunnies and bears. I used to sleep in cars too after long trips. We all did, except Dad. Sometimes I would wake up to see everyone else sleeping while Dad drove. He enjoyed it. He was one of those "got to beat traffic" types. He couldn't wait to get going, and couldn't wait to get home. Occasionally he would drive through the night so we'd be home in the morning to make our ball games or we'd stay an extra day and he would have to get back home to be at work. He never complained about lack of sleep.

The sun was just rising when I pulled into the driveway. I carried Olivia into her room, noticing the stars on her ceiling fading with the sunlight. I brushed her curly hair and tucked her dirty feet inside the blanket and crashed onto my bed. Tanja had left for work just as I got home.

Tanja was surprised to see us home so soon. Olivia told

her with excitement all about the moon and the stars, and asked if she had heard her say good night. Her enthusiasm was contagious. Tanja caught the camping spirit as Olivia urged her to come look at her stars. On the way back to camp, we sang endless choruses of "Twinkle Twinkle Little Star." That night, the three of us marched to the beach, enjoying the solitudes of our own private universe.

When we returned home, Olivia and I launched our starship out of port. She set a course for the first star on the right, and for the rest of the summer, the galaxy was ours.

The Home Front

CARYL K. SILLS

m y sister's attic in the mid-August heat of Cleveland, Ohio, was oppressive.

And the task at hand, while not necessarily unpleasant, was fraught with tensions I hadn't anticipated. Our mother had passed away three months before at age eighty-five. She'd had a long, full, eventually leisured life, and despite the guilt and pain remembering her last days in a nursing home, I might not hope for better for my own eventual exit.

So, here I was, visiting from New Jersey to attend my fortieth high school reunion, and my sister had set aside an hour or so to go through the boxes and bags and albums she'd transferred to her attic when mother's last apartment was taken apart and we new she'd be at the nursing home for whatever time she had left. Furniture had been sold and clothing donated here and there, but we'd hustled mother's personal effects into Lois' attic until we were ready to deal with them.

We certainly weren't ready that hot, sticky morning, but it was time. I sat cross-legged at one end of the attic and Lois plunked herself down at the opposite end. With sad eyes and false bravado, we had agreed to sort through everything, setting aside what we wanted to keep, so that when we met in the middle of the floor, the job would ostensibly be done. But so many photographs. We'd already taken some of my dad's 16-millimeter movies and transferred the good parts to video tape. It added up to about a twenty minute show of a cousin's ice skating conga line with four-year-old me out of control at the end. Then there were short takes of things like Dad waving from his bi-annual Buick or turning a sirloin on the backyard grill. But here, in boxes and albums and photo folders, were so many snapshots, so many. Years back my mother had made duplicates for various family members of some of her favorites, so that at least a few might survive in the back of someone's closet if anything happened to her stash. But even so I was quite unprepared to confront so many memories.

How do you throw a life in pictures away? About twenty years before I had gone to my local photo shop to get more cartridges for our old Airequipt Superba 77 projector. The owner told me the Superba was out of production— everyone was using a slide carousel at that point—but sometimes people asked if he could sell their cartridges once they'd converted to the newer projector. He'd call me.

I picked up the used cartridges and was mildly put out because they came complete with slides. Still, I did not intend to convert all my own slides to a new format, so I was stuck with these little rectangular sleeves into which one inserted a single slide per slot. Inserting the slides was a breeze; removing them could kill a manicure in a matter of seconds. Anyhow, I talked a couple of my sons into helping me and we began pulling slides out of the cartridges and dumping them on the kitchen table. It didn't take long with three set of hands, and the boys took off as soon as the last slide had been plucked. I sat there for an instant and then began to rake the slides into a paper bag so I could put them in the garbage compactor. But I wound up sitting there for a good deal longer (eventually wiping tears out of the corner of my eyes) face to face with someone's life (*someone's whole life!*) spilled across my kitchen table. Where were those cute babies now? Or the smiling men with their arms around a lady or two? Or the old cars and storefronts and beach scenes? How could I throw away someone's whole life? What would happen to all my slides someday? Would some stranger drop them into the garbage, too?

But, of course, I did discard the slides, and here I was being asked to do the same thing with my mother's collection of photographs. I was slightly nauseated, but whether from the heat or the situation, I could only guess that both played a part in my increasing malaise. I told Lois I didn't feel quite well and she glowered. "You promised to help me do this. I'm not having fun either, you know. But all this stuff's a fire hazard and we've got to go through it."

So, okay. I set aside some family photos I wanted to keep and began going through my mother's scrapbooks.

That was even worse. I touched once more the dried corsage from her high school prom, carefully wrapped in cellophane, the one she'd showed me with apologies. "I didn't know Daddy, then," she'd said. I'd wondered if she remembered the boy who'd given it to her, maybe cared for him a little, maybe a lot, but from the dreamy look that came into her eyes, I decided to let the moment pass.

I read menus from her favorite restaurants and invitations to so many weddings and parties and baby showers. And then I came to the newspaper clippings she'd saved, some pasted neatly in an album, and others stuffed into a pocket in the back of the book. For some reason, I wanted to look at those first. It isn't that I'd never seen them before. I must have. But I'd forgotten what they were about. The handful of clippings in my hand covered the years of World War II, and I began to sort through them for the familiar faces of my parents and their friends and neighbors. It was nostalgia of the warmest sort. But all of a sudden I came across a newspaper article from 1943 and I let out a shout, screeching, "Oh, my god!"

"What happened?" Lois asked, getting up quickly to come over to me. "What's the matter? What did you find?"

◄ ►

My mother, Anne R. Klein, was born in 1910 in the town of Wallington, New Jersey, which no longer exists. Its history lies buried beneath the Meadowlands in North Jersey, not far south of Manhattan. Her obituary noted the volunteerism she'd devoted her life to, for the Cystic Fibrosis Foundation and Hadassah, to name a few of her long-standing relationships. She'd knitted and crocheted and sewed just about every article of clothing, from hats and mittens for soldiers overseas in World War II to sweaters and booties for infants immigrating to Israel in more recent times.

Only a few years before her death, she'd agreed to become one of my subjects in a study I was doing on women and leadership. The university where I teach was awarded a grant to conduct the study and develop community-based collaborations to improve opportunities for girls and women. What my mother told me during that taped interview profoundly affected my feelings for her, and I came to a better understanding of myself as well.

Anne had always been my role model. Clever, articulate, and fun-loving, she'd given unselfishly to her family and various good causes, but she'd always expected, and taken, time and space for her own needs and leisure. She was a master balancer. I thought of her as a self-confident and accomplished suburban homemaker. I knew she'd wanted to go back to get a college degree when Lois and I were grown, or at least find an interesting and challenging job. After all, she'd been valedictorian of her high school graduating class when only fifteen. But my dad didn't want her to work. His tradition was that the man provided and the woman nurtured. A working wife would mean he had failed in some way. But he did encourage her to go back to school; only she told me during the interview that she'd never done it because she'd been too scared of failure. I'd always accepted the explanation at the time that she'd been elected to this or that office in one of her organizations and hadn't really had time to do anything else. Now she confessed that she had never seen herself as a leader and wasn't really comfortable being one. She liked to do worthwhile work as long as someone else took the final responsibility and told her what was expected of her. She didn't want to be the boss. Oh, she enjoyed running things, but being in control behind the scenes, so to speak.

I know also, from the obituary that my sister had provided to the local newspapers, that my mother had served as a block captain during World War II and made sure that the lights were turned out or some such thing. It hadn't registered much.

But now I sat, holding in my hands, confirmation of what I had mistaken, even forgotten. After all, I was only seven years old in 1943.

"The Cummings Road Block in Cleveland Heights has been famous since it started," read The Cleveland Press *on Tuesday, August 24, 1943.*

We were one of only few Jewish families on the street. For the most part, that's incidental. My sister and I had close Christian playmates and my mother was on good, friendly terms with most of the neighbors. However, I couldn't go to one of my best friend's birthday party because it was held at the Cleveland Athletic Club which did not allow Jews, and one particularly ugly family, the Jacks, screamed obscenities at Lois and me if one of our alien feet touched a corner of their property. But tragedy and fear make unusual bedfellow.

The block plan, patterned on a model civilian defense promoted by Albert I. Cornsweet, brought together every family on the street to volunteer their time, energy, and expertise wherever it was needed most to keep the home front war effort constantly alive. My favorite family project was our victory garden. Everyone had one in the back yard, and soon these oases spilled over into vacant lots, tended by any and all who volunteered. In fact, each class at the local elementary school worked a small plot in the schoolyard as well. The first green thumb experience with my classmates insured that I would someday have a summer garden of my own and teach my children the joys of it as soon as we could afford our first house. Tomatoes, runner beans, lettuce, carrots—the Taylor Road School victory gardeners raked and watered, tended and tasted, even competed for the biggest tomato or the most beans. I loved every sweaty minute because even the littlest kid knew she was doing something for her country.

The women on our block met once a week to produce bandages and surgical dressings—765 surgical sponges in just one afternoon! Even the men helped box gifts to send to soldiers and sailors overseas, and we all wrote cards and letters to our very own adopted servicemen. Our Cummings Road group had decided to adopt three men from area orphanages: Beech-Brook (Protestant), Parmadale (Catholic), and Bellefaire (my father's Jewish home town). Seventy-four families sent letters and gifts on a regular basis. From the proceeds of its grease collection sales, we even sent a *Reader's Digest* subscription to each of these three adoptees.

At first the group collected thing like cigarettes and razor blades to be distributed by the army as they saw fit. Later, because someone heard that "the boys" needed handkerchiefs, some of the neighbors collected as many as they could. Others on the block worked to fill a large blood bank quota needed for the wounded men who had been returned stateside. My mother and my friends' mothers sometimes served as hostesses and baked cookies for the U.S.O. Letters of appreciation were delivered to the chairwomen of these various committees on a regular basis.

We kids got into the act by colleting grease and cans for the grease salvage program. We went door to door to collect from neighbors, and then took the grease to one of two houses at either end of the street. There, the women of the houses melted the grease and poured it into the cleaned cans, which were then turned in at the local butcher shop. This was the fun part for the collectors, transporting the grease cans in our wagons or, after a snowfall, on our sleds.

There was a great little hill going down to Taylor Road, the main shopping streets in our bustling suburb. We'd trudge back up the hill after each delivery, taking turns riding or pulling each other along. Each kid had at least one pocket full of candy bought with "appreciation" money from a mother or two.

I remember, too, that practically every Cummings Road family regularly displayed the American flag as a symbol of solidarity with their sons and brothers and fathers at war. We learned what other block groups were doing from newspaper accounts, but also one of the senior air wardens put up a bulletin board on his front lawn for notices of general interest. A pennant was flown from the top of this board to announce meetings of our Cummings Road Neighbor Front, meetings that were well attended and usually productive. We even had a bi-weekly newsletter, sent to our adopted servicemen as well, to keep them current on home front news.

Every so often, block organizations teamed up to raise funds for civilian defense. One such success was a carnival we held with the Grosvenor Block that raised $700, increased everyone's awareness of our purpose and goals, and proved to be a heck of a lot of fun. ("Heck" was one of those words we said back then when our mothers weren't listening.)

One newspaper article mentioned the Cummings Road Block Volunteers as a model "of what can be done by organized group in keeping the home front war effort constantly alive." Moreover, "civilian war work is not something that is discussed just once a month. It is something done every day of the week, in one way or another."

And that is how I remember my mother, always joining to help someone, someplace. The photo of her and my friends' mothers, in that 1943 newspaper article, touches my memory with pride and thankfulness. My childhood was rich and caring despite the war at its center.

I was also very proud of my father. He was the Cummings Road Block air warden. He hadn't been called to serve because he was married with two children and because he was asthmatic. But I remember how he looked in his helmet and flashlight, tall and dignified and incredibly handsome while saving the world. He'd come into my sister's bedroom and pull down the blackout shades and then kiss us good night before he strode through the neighborhood instructing others on what to do, and making sure everyone complied with the rules. Not one tiny glimmer would shine from Cummings Road to tell the German pilots that we were there!

I wasn't too young to understand much of what was happening in Europe and Asia. I read the newspapers, I listened to the adults talking about the war, and with my friends, I tried to make sense of so much hate "over there" and so much compassion and collaboration in my own small world. Why couldn't everyone be like my parents,

why couldn't every kid have a father as grand and important as my own!

◄ ►

"What did you find?" Lois' voice brought me back from my
memories. I showed her the newspaper article and the
photo of the familiar, tall handsome man in the helmet,
holding a flashlight. But it was not our father.

It was our mother!

Could it be the same Anne Klein who said she didn't
want to be a leader, that she was much more comfortable
behind the scenes? She'd always been a wife who deferred
to her husband because she'd been brought up with the
traditional model of marriage. My father mostly treated her
like a queen and, like she said, she was comfortable knowing
what was expected of her.

But during the World War II blackouts, this woman
became the community watcher, the one who accepted the
awesome job of seeing that everyone—even those who
didn't like her religion or her face—complied with the
cooperation our government expected and needed if we
were to survive. For that brief time, my mother controlled
light. It appeared or disappeared because she made it happen. And when the war was over, she rarely mentioned it.
And if she did, well, it was no big deal. "We all pitched in,"
she'd probably say.

The friendships forged on Cummings Road during
those meetings and projects for the war effort lasted even

after many of the families had moved away. We did keep in touch for years, but then, as happens, the contact became less and less and then it was gone. The memories, on the other hand, are forever.

When I ask myself now how I came to be who I am, how I had the guts to think that an average, youngest sibling, spoiled little princess could aspire to become a university professor, I know that my mother's genes have been busy. Mother's goals were very different than mine, but when she was needed, she was always there 100%. And it was always, no big deal. But having Anne as a role model has been, indeed, a very big deal.

Solid Ground

COOPER GALLEGOS

my mother is making borscht, following a recipe from *Women's Day*. Her bunioned feet are splayed out on the flowered linoleum, the elbows of her nightgown soaked in red. Beets are splattered against the yellow kitchen walls and drip down toward the dusty molding at the floor. It's hard to tell the red, beet-stained walls apart from the blood-stained hallway where my mother slipped and fell last week. They look the same. My mother is not a cook. This is a spur-of-the-moment thing and the beets have gotten the upper hand.

My mother calls herself a craft person. I think of her as a creator of chaos. Everywhere she goes she swirls up a cloud of confusion. When she gets me alone she says things like, "You are my favorite child." Her eyes drift around like she's embarrassed by this, but I think she's trying to divide and conquer. The three of us are too much to swallow. My older brother is under psychiatric care, although the psychiatrist is a family friend who talks to my brother over cocktails. My mother is putting a lot of stock into this friend to turn my sullen brother around. If you ask me it's my mother who needs the psychiatric care. She's given to moods that swing from one extreme to the

other. Our square stucco house is full of her mental wan-
derings. The walls are covered with her handmade masks
and five-foot abstract oil paintings. Her bedroom is a bliz-
zard of paper cranes she's folding into a peace monument.
One thousand paper cranes she says will bring about world
peace. Most of the time she's folding the origami paper
she's wailing or screaming. If you ask me, peace should
begin at home.

"You're going to catch polio with those bare feet!" My
mother has come around the corner of the kitchen into the
living room where I'm lulled into a trance by the TV. I've
dug my bare feet deep into the chocolate shag rug. I've
buried my stubbed toe into the dusty pile searching out the
polio virus, seeking the illness that might bring me some
kind of quiet. My two brothers, Gerald and Tim, burrow in
deeper too. My father is like an inanimate object, a boulder
wedged into the crease of the couch, the dust of the day
accumulating on his shoulders. "Polio! Is that what you all
want?" She seems to have forgotten the borscht. My
father's head sinks into his shoulders and suddenly we're
all real interested in The Lone Ranger who charges to the
center of the 10-inch TV screen and rears up on his horse,
the huge horse penis taking center stage. "Okay! That's that
then!" My mother stalks through the living room, down
the hallway stained with her blood, and slams the door to
her bedroom.

In the middle of the night I bump into my mentally ill

brother at the open refrigerator door. He's sucking the pimentos out of the green olives. No one has gone near the borscht. The red remains still drip down the front of the stove. "I'm never going to eat beets. Not after this." I point dramatically toward the mess. It looks like a crime scene. It looks like our life. Gerald grunts. We're like hunters and gatherers. I poke my head into the refrigerator and grab a raw hotdog and head back to our room leaving Gerald who is swigging the last of the olive juice from the rust-rimmed jar.

During the school year our school bus grinds up Porter Street where, at the top of the hill, the driver shifts gears and the bus coughs and spits out black exhaust. It pauses in its struggle right in front of the heavy wooden gates to Sister Kinney's Home for Polio Victims. All year I've been standing on the tips of my oxford toes to catch a glimpse through the limbs of the pepper tree and into the windows where children languish in iron lungs and wheelchairs. Where each breath is cause for celebration, each step applauded by the long thin hands of the nuns. I picture those hands gently cupping my chin. "My, we're doing better today, aren't we?" they say and my eyes slide across the bare white walls, and I'm left alone to soak in the silence and the one-dimensional order of my days. I long for the freedom of Sister Kinney's Home, with its huge molding monolithic building, and that pepper tree whose branches sweep away the traces of disease every time the breeze shifts. I see this polio virus as my one way out of the inevitable legacy my mother seems intent on leaving me, her only daughter. The thought of illness frees me to be anything I want to be. Frees me from the future my mother insists is mine.

"You're like me, aren't you? Same vivid imagination. You can be anything you want to be, Jeanie," she says in the dusty squalor of her bedroom. She's called me in the day after the refrigerator raid. I'm bleary-eyed and heavy with fatigue. She's still in bed wrapped in nothing but a sheet. Bits of red yarn, coming unraveled from some blanket she's weaving, lie in strands across the yellow-white of the sheet. I'm not brave enough to say, "Is this what you wanted to be?" I think it but can't say it. I can't really figure out how all of us could possibly figure into my mother's great plan for herself. Every day she's on to something new. Today, she's heaved back against her pillow, one arm draped across her eyes like the sight of me is more than she can bear. "I wanted to be a writer," she says. "I still could be." I nod but in her self-inflicted blindness she can't see me. The sun is pouring in between the slats of the Venetian blinds, throwing bars of light across her body. She looks like a prisoner pinned there on her bed. Suddenly she flings her arm away from her eyes and looks directly at me. And in that moment with the light just right I can see a glimmer of what might be love coming from her. She looks away quickly without giving me what I need. Without saying,

"Jeanie, I love you," or touching my hand. It's as if these intimate words and gestures might bind us together, might cause some sort of chain reaction that she just won't be able to sustain. Her looking away is the break I need to slip out of her bedroom, through the stained hall and out the back door to the tangled green of our summer yard. Just in the nick of time. I'm lucky really to have gotten away. I could just as easily have sunk to the bottom of the rubble there in her room, crushed by the bones of my mother, never seeing the light of day again.

Nighttime is the best time. It's the time when the differences between us and the rest of the world are least noticeable. The darkness evens the score. I'm wild when I kick the can high over Susan Ord's shingled roof. The can crashes onto their front porch and Susan's father slams out of the screen door and yells for his kids to come in. Gerald and Tim and I lay belly-deep in the weeds that line the outer fringe of the Ord property. The neighborhood is dying down. The luster has gone out. The sheen on the blacktop has dulled. Porch lights switch off. The three of us are on our own. Finally, when the moon is hovering above the houses and its light lies in the thicket of walnut tree branches, Susan and Gary and Janis and Dennis and Diane and all the other kids are sound asleep in their houses, the ones with the trimmed hedges. Meanwhile, the three of us are still loose jointed and barefoot wandering around the neighborhood, feral, picking at any tidbits left in the wake of the day.

I don't know whether to call this freedom. It seems loose bottomed and precarious. I can't yet grasp that it might be setting my mind free, building antibodies against convention and structure. I don't yet see these late night forages as the pubescent landscape of opportunity.

When Tim and Gerald are finally snorting in their sleep I plan my escape. I've got to make a break for it if I'm going to make it to adulthood. I lie gasping in the lower bunk, sure I can feel the slow paralysis of the virus creeping up from my wounded toe, encircling my leg, tightening around my ribs. I feel a moment of regret but I shrug it off with a valiant breath. I am ready for the danger of estrangement. I feel courage well up in my chest. Tomorrow morning before the sun has warmed the air, while shadows still slide across the neighborhood, I'll ride my bike up Porter Street. My sturdy legs will pump with everything I've got, and there in the light, just before the sun breaks through, with my heavy braids and my vivid imagination, I'll make it to solid ground. I'll pedal through the gravel and bits of mica along the road until I reach the top where the school bus always pauses to shift gears, a girl of determination and valor. I'll slide right up to the heavy wooden doors of Sister Kinney and demand to be let in.

◄►

It is thirty years later, long after we have all escaped, slipping through her fingers like so many undone projects. I'm foraging at our local flea market. I've spent a lifetime perfecting my foraging skills until I'm an expert. I see my mother on the cover of an *Arizona Highways* magazine. There is a stack of them on a vendor's unsteady card table. He sees me scrutinizing his dilapidated collection and he gets up laboriously from the metal step of his battered camper and flicks his cigarette onto the blacktop. "Fifty cents," he says. He's got the watery eyes and drooping jowls of a man who's spent a lifetime in the sun on meager rations. I see a desert rat. I see a contemporary of my mother.

It is thirty years after my mother is found in her room of crafts by a neighbor, all the color gone out of her body as if it were sucked dry by the energy of her leaving. She still clutched the brown plastic prescription bottle of barbiturates, her body light like the husk of an insect.

I see my mother in the landscape that stretches across the cover of *Arizona Highways*, in the broad sweep of sky that blends into the soft curve of distant mountains. I see her suddenly striding in her heavy hiking boots through the strewn rubble of rock that leads toward a river bed, pickaxe in hand, pith helmet slightly askew, picking up debris left millions of years ago by the glaciers that wound through the Cochise Valley, and I feel a sudden stroke of luck. This woman whose life was a wreck of experience had a gift that she was always on her way to delivering to me.

For years I've carried around the burden of my mother, hauling her bones piggyback, the spirit of her chaffing against the current of my days, the rawboned anguish of her life just below the surface of everything I do. It hits me, there in the flea market aisle with the desert rat patiently waiting for me to plunk down fifty cents for one of his magazines. The reckless energy that was the pulse of our house was simply her mad attempt to find her way out of our neighborhood, a place of meatloaf dinners and sponge cake desserts. I hardly know who I am without this baggage. Surely I'll float away, untethered by this anchor of sorrow. It's the thing that grounds me. When the first recognition of my mother's real legacy seeps into my consciousness I am astounded. It's like gulping pure oxygen. As I plow my way up one flea market row after another, searching for the exact piece of rock to complete the sculpture I'm creating, I see how well I've received her gift. Long after she is lying in her bed with her bony hands around the brown plastic bottle of pills, when she had decided that no, this is not what she wanted to be, I find myself the grateful inheritor.

My mother never found her solid ground but maybe that's not what she was looking for. Maybe she was trying to teach me that creativity and even joy is best found in the hidden fissures of an uneven life. And even though I can still smell the scent of blood in the air, I see too the promise in a clear morning with nothing between me and the world but my imagination, and I know I am one of the lucky ones.

Doctor Jones
and the One Percent Solution

PIROOZ M. KALAYEH

y dad called on Tuesday. He started with his custom-ary, "Doctor Jones," a nickname he had called me, on and off, since high school when we saw *Indiana Jones and The Last Crusade* together. He was convinced he was Sean Connery, and whenever I would get mad at him, he would reference the movie—"Let it go, Indiana," he would say. It was later, after we hadn't talked for a couple years, that he started calling me Doctor Jones on a regular basis. I guess "let it go" got old, or I graduated to a new status, because now I was in school and not wasting my life playing rock 'n' roll, or "that drug business," as he called it. Of course, my father told friends it was because he wanted me to be a doctor and he wasn't going to stop until it happened.

"I will call him Doctor Jones until it happens."

I have about six messages at all times that start with Doctor Jones. Sometimes he draws out the vowels like we haven't talked in years—"Doctor Jooones," or "Heeey, Doctor Jones, how are you man?" I would usually call him back in those cases, because I knew he was in a good mood, and it would be bearable, but as soon as he started with a "Hey" pronounced "Eh," and swallowed the "S" with his accent, I knew it would be a long one.

"Eh, Doctor Jones."

"Hey, Dad," I said.

"How's life?"

"It's good…"

"Good is good and bad is bad."

Damn. I had just finished my application to Princeton's Fellowship Program and was hoping I could break his run. Words like "Princeton" excited him. He would say, "You are on the path, man," and describe his interest in other words like *science* and *math*, or revert to his old favorite, *SAT*, but he was currently stuck on the catch phrase, "Good is good and bad is bad," and had used it in our past sixteen phone conversations.

Seventeen.

It had a paralyzing effect. I couldn't really respond to it. How can you? Sure, good is good and bad is bad, but what does it mean? One of my old rock buddies calls these moments, "Pomerisms," because Pome was my nickname back in the day, and I made the same grandiose statements that halted conversation and created awkward silences, except when I did it, you wouldn't be filled with dread. They were usually some kind of joke. Someone would be talking about the weather or girl troubles and I'd say, "Your mama" or "vagina," or tell journalists, "I was brought to Earth to destroy all cover bands."

We sat in silence for a couple minutes before he threw out a few of his favorite love proverbs.

"I swim the twenty-six-mile poison river when I see your embracing arm. I need very little to be the mountain, to be unbeatable."

"What are you talking about?" I said.

"One day when you have children you'll know what I'm talking about," he paused. "I become drunk when I eat one raisin from your garden. I become an eagle when you call my name."

I have no idea why he talks like this. It usually makes me mad. He doesn't know a thing about love. When I told him I was getting married last July, he told me I was crazy. He said, "What are you talking?" and then hung up. I don't know if he was angry that I was marrying an American girl, or what? I just sat there wondering why I even bothered. It took a couple of months before he progressed to, "Are you sure?"

Now that I'm married he still asks if I'm happy.

"Are you happy?" he says.

"Yeah, Dad."

"Good. That is good."

"Well, good is good and bad is bad, right Dad?"

"That's right," he says.

My wife would just laugh when I told her.

"What else can you do?"

"I guess, you're right."

"Don't let him get to you, baby."

It's been easier with my mom. Last weekend before she got on the phone I heard her customary, "You are crazy." Ordinarily, it would make me cringe. But this time I imagined my mother as Jerry Seinfeld. She's back behind the curtain screaming, "You are karazee" in her thick Persian accent and then walks on stage.

I was laughing when she got on the phone.

"Hossein, eh? Are you laughing?"

"That's so funny, Mom. Every time I get on the phone I can hear you coming, because the first thing you say is, 'You are karazee.'"

"Boy, let me tell you what he did. He came into the bathroom..."

I lost it right there. I still had the image of my mother as Jerry Seinfeld, screaming, "You are karazee," and now she follows it with the perfect transition, "Boy, let me tell you what he did."

I told her she could take her act on the road and probably make millions off it.

She started to laugh, "Oh, come on, Hossein."

"Yeah, Mom, you'll be famous."

"Come on."

"You'll make millions. Your name will be in lights. Can't you see it?"

Then as soon as I thought she realized how ridiculous she sounded, she stops laughing and continues the story.

"No, *ree-lee* Hossein, let me tell you what he did. He came and banged the door. Boom-boom. Oh Hossein, I am telling you I got so scared. I was in the bathroom, and this boy comes just like that. Is not right!"

I laughed for about ten minutes. I told my brother about it, and he said I should set up a mike on Main Street and do impersonations. I told him I didn't know. "Right now, it's just good not to take Mom too seriously."

I thought about that conversation, as my father started his "This is *your* time" speech: "This is *your* time, man. All the time you need to be in a state of Kundalini. Life is just so precious. People shoot you from left and right. Is tough, man. You have to be like a rock. No one can move you."

Over the years I have heard several versions of it, and it has stayed true to its original 1980-1981 form, except for some minor alterations in self-help terminology, such as "Kundalini," which were added as my father amassed a rather large collection of books by Deepak Chopra and M. Scott Peck, M.D. They usually came to him as unwanted gifts that he would get for my brothers or me.

Last year I got *The Seven Paths to Highly Effective People*.
"You like it?" My dad asked.

"Yeah, thanks." I put the book down, and within a week it was on his bookshelf.

"Isn't that my book, Dad," I would ask later.

"Oh no, is mine."

When I graduated high school, it was the same thing.

He had promised a present I could use. The way he said it, I was expecting a car or money, something big.

"I get you a good present. You can use," he said.

When I walked out of the ceremony to the parking lot, I looked around for the car. *It's got to be here,* I thought. Then I saw my father standing there in the middle of the lot, proud, and holding a gift in his hand.

I knew it was a watch before I opened it. My older brother had gotten a watch when he graduated, and I knew that my father had a collection of leftovers. I figured it was the same one.

I was right.

"Thanks, Dad," I said. Within a week it was back in his closet, where he kept his special things: his medals from running marathons, a collection of watches and leather jackets he had gotten as gifts, or bought for himself, and the drawing I did when I was twelve.

He would look at the drawing and say, "Remember when you did this? You see what a good father I am. I keep this thing." Then he would say how good I was when I was five, "When you were five, it was the best time of your life. We had the best time."

As opposed to now, when I wasn't five anymore, I guess. Now I had changed with the "drug business" and getting married, so I wasn't surprised when I graduated college and got the same watch again. I didn't even say anything. I just put it on. He waited for me to take it off, but I wasn't going to. I was keeping it this time.

I looked over at my watch on the dresser. He was now on neuron clusters: "Every person in this universe has a reflection of you inside his brain, in this cluster of neurons. If all the time there are bad memories, is not a rose garden."

"I hear you," I said.

"I hope you enjoy your life and do your best every day."

Okay, Dad. Good talking to you, I got ready to say, but the engine just coughed and kept going.

"Remember that movie we saw together?"

"Which one?"

"The one where the guy say, 'Freedom, freedom!'"

"Oh, *Braveheart*, Dad."

I picked up the watch from the dresser and walked outside with the phone. It was snowing. A couple of flakes landed on the watch's face. I had never seen ones that big. They were beautiful. I touched one with my finger and lifted it to my face. It looked so perfect.

"Yeah, with just a few sentences he brought the people, his leadership together," he paused, straight into Polonius, and I heard Hamlet in my mind, *"Dead, for a ducat, dead!"*

"My advice to you is always be impeccable. Whatever you do, make no assumption about anybody. Do your best every moment. I love you, man. God bless you. I hope you get whatever you desire. God will give you what you want, I know."

"How do you know?"

"I know, man. We are only using one percent of what we're capable. I know because part of me is inside you. Love is not a simple word. It has physical molecules. When I say I love you there are a hundred thousand neurons associated with you in my brain. When you say I love you, you have to say it impeccable, so those neurons hear it. If you don't tune it, you don't receive it, so you don't fulfill your potential."

"That's great, Dad," I said, as I stepped inside and closed the sliding door.

My wife was on the couch. *Trading Rooms* was on, her favorite. She looked up from the television.

"Who are you talking to?" she whispered.

"My dad," I told her with a smile, as he continued:

"Did I tell the story about the turtle and the scorpion?"

"No, tell me the story about the turtle and the scorpion."

This was going to be good. I could tell. My father's stories were much more bearable. When I was a kid he told me hundreds of these fables, and I was sure he had told this one too, but they changed every time.

"This is the story about a scorpion that's so powerful. Once upon a time this scorpion, he was going to a temple. This scorpion was just like a person. I tell you this because this story is really about people. Some people are like a scorpion and some people are like a dog."

I could hear him translating the Farsi in his head.

"So once upon a time there was a story about a scorpion. He was going to a temple and there was a river, and turtle was going the same direction, so the scorpion said, 'How about you give me a ride and take me to the other side?' And the turtle said, 'Well you have to promise me that you don't hit me with'—what is that thing called the scorpion get you with?"

"A stinger?"

"Yeah, so he say, 'You have to promise not to get me with the stinger and I die,' so the scorpion say okay, and walk on his back. Then when they get a little bit in the middle of the river, scorpion put the stinger in the back of the turtle. Turtle say, 'Hey man, what are you doing? I give you this ride and you are putting a poison in my back.' And scorpion say, 'Let me see, if I am stinging you, putting a poison in your back, is my habit.'"

He stopped to explain, "Some people are like that. No matter what you do."

"Okay, then what?"

"Suddenly the turtle went under the water and the scorpion scream, 'You promise you take me on the other side, but now when you go down, the water is taking me.' Turtle said, 'This is my nature.'"

"Great story, Dad."

"...Yeah, so remember no matter what you do, even if you're Hitler you can't change people. Even if you love them to death you can't change people. Maybe if you're like a Jesus you can change people..."

He thought about that for a few seconds.

"Forget about changing people. You can't change people. Take nothing personally. Do your best. Ask yourself everyday if you're happy, and if you're not, you have to go back to square one. Get mentally intelligent, spiritually intelligent.

"I never talk like this with anybody, not because I want to give a lecture or anything, sometime you are my son, sometime you get a little bit deeper ... My principle is 99 percent of our essence is the same. I came to this conclusion, not because I read books. So when I say part of you is inside me, part of me is inside you."

I could feel it end there. It was as if he was waiting to get to that last line.

"Okay, Doctor Jones, I have to go. You take care of yourself and keep your eyes on the prize."

"Okay, Dad. I'll talk to you soon." I hung up the phone and sat on the couch. I let out a deep sigh, "Baby, you won't believe some of the things I just got."

"Juicy, huh?"

"You have no idea."

"Well, go write it down."

"I will." I looked down at the watch in my hands. It had stopped.

There Is Always a Way

OPAL PALMER ADISA

my mother lived her life without malice and never paused to lament about setbacks. Instead she forged ahead, finding alternatives, living her favorite motto, "Where there is a will there is a way." I had not known how much like my mother I had become until about seven years ago when I got divorced and found myself left with three children to support and raise. I was determined not to alter my lifestyle or deprive my children of opportunities. Whenever I felt overcome by bills or fatigue, I would say to myself, "Where there is a will there is a way," and doors and opportunities would open for both my children and me. My mother's proverbs were my mantras.

"There is more than one way to skin a cat," my mother hissed, depressing the accelerator and the car sped down the two-lane street as if it was the only vehicle on the narrow road. Both my mother's hands grasped the steering wheel and she was leaning into it, her eyes straight ahead. I kept glancing on the road before us and at her. I held my breath, hoping I would not explode. I had never witnessed my mother so angry with her youngest brother, my favorite uncle. Their raised voices had arrested me in the backyard where I played with my infant cousins.

"What do you mean, you can't do it today? I said I was going to ask someone else and you said no need to pay someone for what you could easily do."

"Chu, Cathy. It can wait till next week. I've got to make a run."

Suddenly my mother's humming intruded on my recall of the recent altercation with her brother. She was humming a hymn, interspersed with a few words of the song; soon her voice was full, taking liberty with the tune, until she filled up all the space in the car. I stuck my head out the open window and breathed.

"Don't hang out that window," she warned, picking up the rhythm of the song with ease. I turned fully in my seat to look at her face. She was smiling, the same wide-teeth grin that made her face appear to glow and I knew she wasn't angry anymore, not at Uncle Seymour, not at anyone. I joined her in singing a song that marked the beginning of many mornings. My mother often sang me awake, her voice strong and persistent as the sun.

By the time we had gone through the song twice, my mother had slowed her speed but only slightly because she always drove fast, speeding past other cars.

"Where are we going, Mommy?" I felt it was now safe to ask as she was sitting relaxed in her seat.

"Miss Mac," she replied, glancing at me. I didn't ask her why we were going to her best friend when we had only planned to visit Uncle Seymour, where I had hoped to spend most of the afternoon, playing with my two young cousins. At nine years old, I knew from experience that my mother would only tell me what she felt I needed to know. She would not discuss the details of the quarrel between her younger brother and herself, except to refer to it as "grown-up business." Still I felt the air light enough to broach the subject.

"Mommy, are we going back to Uncle Seymour?"

"No," she said flatly.

I kept quiet, hoping she would say more. She slowed and turned onto a familiar street. We were not far from Miss Mac's house, with its sprawling yard, way back from the street, five dogs, and numerous fruit trees. Tamarind was in season, so undoubtedly Miss Mac would give me a large bag to pick enough to take home so Mommy could make tamarind-ball and the tart drink that I loved. Meanwhile, they could talk without me eavesdropping, and her dogs would sniff at my feet and at the tamarind lying on the ground.

"Opie," my mother's gentle voice brought me back to the present, "your uncle and I aren't seeing eye to eye now, but remember, there is always more than one way to skin a cat. He thinks because I needed his help, I have to be inconvenienced. No sir," Mommy ended flatly. I had heard that tone before. I had all too often witnessed my mother willing the wind to stop for her, and more often than not it paused and allowed her to accomplish some task. She was generous to a fault, fiercely independent, and did not take kindly to anyone who did not keep his or her word or who reneged on a promised favor. I deduced that was what had happened between her and Uncle Seymour, because I remembered him saying that if she came by his house Saturday afternoon, like we had done, that he would go with her to get something. That was why I had thought I would have been spending the afternoon with my cousins and my uncle's dimpled wife, Trisha.

Mommy stopped in front of Miss Mac's gate and blew the horn. The gardener opened the gate and we drove down the long path, the dogs racing and barking at the car. Then we turned left and parked just beyond the wide-columned steps leading to the expansive wrap-around veranda. Miss Mac was rocking on the veranda, and even before the car stopped, she climbed down the stairs and opened my door. As I stepped out, she hugged me in her fleshy arms, burying my face in her bosom.

"Cathy, what a pleasant surprise," she said, releasing me and turning to my mother. "Shush dogs, shush," she said, slapping at the side of her leg and turning to the dogs that were still barking. She ordered them with a sharp voice and clapped her hands together, "Go sit down! Go!" The five dogs paused, angled their heads, and then slowly walked off, wagging their tails.

"Cathy, I was just sitting down to a tall glass of home-made cherry juice. Come and join me. It is such a hot day."

Mommy and Miss Mac embraced, and then climbed the steps leading to the veranda. I followed at their heels. "Opal, you go in the kitchen and help yourselves to two raisin cookies that I just made, and bring two glasses." Before I was halfway through the door, I heard Miss Mac ask my mother, "So Cathy, what brings you here this afternoon? I thought…" I dared not linger so I did not hear my mother's response.

As I had suspected, as soon as I was done with my cookies and juice, I was told to get a bag from the kitchen and go and collect tamarinds to take home. The gardener was asked to pull some from the tallest branches. I wandered around the yard, playing more with the dogs than collecting tamarinds, and glancing every so often to the veranda to steal a look at my mother. I wondered how long we would be staying? I was curious to learn which cat my mother intended to skin and why. Perhaps that's why we didn't have cats. I felt sick just thinking about my mother skinning a cat. I convinced myself that she would never skin a cat just because she was mad at Uncle Seymour.

Mommy was always using proverbs to teach me a lesson. Most times they had nothing to do with the things I thought, and half of them made no sense to me. About a half-hour lapsed, the sun unrelenting, my shirt sticking to my back. By now I had filled up a big bag of tamarind and still many lay on the ground.

Just as I had decided to walk back to the shade of the

veranda, a pickup truck stopped by the gate and blew its horn. I turned to see if I recognized the man driving, but I didn't. Miss Mac did not call to me to open the gate, so I sauntered toward the veranda, dragging the large bag with tamarinds. Mommy and Miss Mac were walking swiftly toward me, and we met mid-way between the gate and the veranda.

"Be a good girl, and listen to Miss Mac," Mommy said, hugging me quickly and kissing me on the cheek. "I'm going to get something. Shouldn't be gone for more than an hour or so." Before I could collect my thoughts, she and Miss Mac were walking toward the gate and talking fast. I stood where they left me, feeling lost and alone. I saw Miss Mac talking to the man in the pickup truck, and then watched Mommy get in the front with the man and then they drove off. My heart dropped to my feet like a big coconut that I would never be able to pick up. I didn't know the man who Mommy drove off with, smiling. I had never seen him before. Immediately another of my mother's maxims popped into my head: "Not every skinned teeth is laughter." Maybe my mother wasn't really smiling. Maybe that man was taking her away from me.

It seemed like a very long time before Miss Mac stopped scolding the dogs and walked back to where I was rooted. I don't know if she saw my heart at my feet and felt sorry for me, but I knew she was hugging me and she took the bag out of my hand.

"Is you worrying? Your Mommy come back soon; she has to collect something, and my friend Mr. Taylor is helping her out. He has a daughter about your age. I should have told him to bring her to keep you company. But not to worry, you can help me shell these tamarinds. But first we will pick some cherries from the back. The trees are full," Miss Mac said, taking my hand.

I could feel my heart trying to pick itself up from off my feet.

"Come Little Miss Cathy," Miss Mac said, pinching my cheeks, "Mommy soon come."

Usually I loved it when Miss Mac called me Little Miss Cathy. She never tired of saying I was the spitting image of my mother, hence her nickname for me. But now with my mother gone with that man, I wondered if she was calling me Miss Cathy because Mommy wasn't going to be coming back. I allowed Miss Mac to hold my hand and lead me to the back, but my feet dragged like a wet towel being pulled through the sand. All the while we picked cherries I kept chanting inside my head another of my mother's sayings, "After the rain, the sun is bound to come out." I understood this phrase and always shouted it after an afternoon summer shower as I ran back outside to finish my play. Mommy was the sun and that mean man, Mr. Taylor, was the rain that was keeping my mommy away. After picking two large bags of cherries, Miss Mac and I went into the kitchen where we sat in the cool, taking off the brittle brown skin from the tamarinds, and de-seeding them in preparation to make tamarind juice. It seemed like forever since my mother had left. Miss Mac was telling me how she made tamarind juice, but that was not how Mommy made hers, so I looked at her and said, "Miss Mac, there is more than one way to cook chicken." She looked at me a little puzzled like I often look at Mommy when she says something like that. Then she smiled and said, "There sure is more than one way, Little Miss Cathy."

I smiled and felt my heart crawling up my knee. Shortly after, my mother burst into the kitchen, smiling. She handed me two small brown bags of warm peanuts that I loved. I threw my arms around her neck and squealed. "Mommy! You are back! Thank you," I said opening the packet of peanuts and feeling my heart beating in my chest.

"So Cathy, you got it?"

"Yes. There was lots of traffic—that's why we took so long. Mr. Taylor made sure they wrapped it well so it wouldn't get scratched. He went home to have lunch. Said he would be back in an hour."

"Well Cathy, you must be hungry yourself. I was about to make some sandwiches," Miss Mac said, heading toward the bread box.

"I brought us patties and coco bread. I left them in the dining room. We just need some juice. Let me go and wash my hands."

"You must have read my mind," Miss Mac laughed. "I was just thinking I had a taste for patties. I will get plates and juice."

"Mommy, look how many tamarinds Miss Mac and I shelled. And we collected cherries too for us to take home."

"I see you've been working hard," my mother smiled, heading down the hallway toward the bathroom.

Mr. Taylor returned two hours later with a great big box in the back of his pickup and a little girl, with small eyes and hair braided neatly in cornrows, bouncing beside him in the front of the pickup. Mommy and I hugged and bade Miss Mac good-bye and got in our car with Mr. Taylor following behind. Several times I had to remind my mother to slow down because I could not see the pickup behind us. When we got to our house, Mr. Taylor said to Mommy, "Miss Catherine, I see your foot don't spare the gas. You drive like a mini-bus driver. You dangerous on the road!" He laughed and wiped his brow with his handkerchief. My mother laughed and invited him into the house. Then turning to glance at me, she said seriously, "Manners and good breeding live in the same house." Then, seeing my baffled look, Mommy commanded, "Introduce yourself and offer her some juice," indicating Mr. Taylor's daughter who was still sitting in the truck.

"Mabel, you can come out and play, just mind yourself," Mr. Taylor said to his daughter as he stepped over the threshold.

The sun had set before Mr. Taylor and Mabel left. She and I had stayed outside the entire time, playing hopscotch and jumping rope. Our next-door neighbor, Mr. Williams, had come over to help Mr. Taylor lift the box from off his pickup truck, and I heard furniture being moved around. But still I had no idea what my mother had bought. I didn't think our house could hold anything else, as every room was packed with large, dark mahogany furniture that I had to polish and dust, but at that time my concern was on play.

After we waved good-bye to Mr. Taylor and Mabel, my mother led me into the living room, and right where the armchair and table used to be by the window there now stood a shiny rectangular structure, wider than the width of my outstretched arms and the height was just above my waist. I ran my finger over the top. "It's very pretty, Mommy," I said looking down at my reflection in the shiny surface. "What is it?"

"You like it?" she asked, reaching for a stack of records. She fished through the records, found what she was looking for, then raised the top of the rectangular box, and I saw the turntable. She put on a record and Fats Domino's voice blared, and we danced around the room. We both clapped when the song ended. As my mother showed me how to stack the records, and tune the radio stations, I ran my hand over the word "Grundig," the brand of stereo components that was new on the market.

That evening, as we ate supper, my mother said to me,

"Just remember there is always a way, and always keep your word; don't make a promise if you think you won't be able to keep your word."

Two weeks later Uncle Seymour was back at our house with my cousins. My mother stacked the stereo with records, turned up the volume, and we all danced around. My mother never mentioned the quarrel they had; it was as if it had never happened. But just before Uncle Seymour left, as he hugged her, I heard him say, "Sorry Sis, I know how you are about promises."

"Your word must be as good as your spit," Mommy replied, hugging her brother and bidding him a safe drive home.

I value my mother, and because I witnessed her keeping her word, sometimes at great personal inconvenience, I do not make promises lightly. I keep my word to my children, friends, and colleagues. But mostly, I keep my word to myself, honoring what's best in me. Like my mother, I believe one's word should be "as good as his or her spit."

That's How It Is
with My Mother

JENNIFER ROBINSON

the first Thursday starts out by accident. My mother calls me out of the blue, we talk about nothing for about ten minutes, and eventually she persuades me to meet her at the Chinese restaurant five blocks away from my apartment building. We have never had a close relationship so I am surprised. The plan is for twelve o'clock. Her theory is that the lunch rush really begins at twelve-thirty, and so by getting there at noon exactly we will be free of huge crowds that start pouring through the door in droves.

When I step inside the plush restaurant, the coolness of the room overwhelms me. I feel as though the walls are closing in. Then I look to my left and she's standing right behind me. We are exactly the same height. People have always said we look alike, too. She has said she wants to discuss my divorce. I have told her it's the last thing I want to talk about.

The hostess smiles and nods at us. "Two of you?" she asks politely, holding two burgundy menus with dragons wrapped around their slim spines. "Yes," I say, and she leads us to our booth, which is way at the very end and faces the kitchen.

"That dress makes you look very slim from the back. Very flattering," my mother says from behind me. I slide into the booth easily, hiding myself from her. I have never been good at taking compliments. I notice she has gotten her long blond hair cut and is wearing a new type of eye makeup, which makes her eyes look bigger and bolder. I have dressed carefully to impress her and I am secretly glad she likes what I'm wearing. The waitress smiles and walks off.

I hold the menu in front of me, blocking her entirely from view. "Jessica Ann," she says in her motherly voice, "That's rude. Put the menu down." I feel like I'm seven years old.

"Sorry," I mumble. I am nervous because I don't want to talk about the divorce and because I don't know what's going to come out of her mouth. I watch her eyes roam the menu. "I think I'll try the Kung Pao chicken," she finally announces. "What about you?"

I feel too numb to eat. "I guess I'll get the chicken in peanut sauce."

"Good choice." She closes the giant menu, sets it in front of her and crosses her arms, giving me her full attention. "Well?" She reminds me of a giant statue.

"Well what?" I ask.

"You know what I'm talking about. Don't play dumb.

You and Joe? The divorce? I want to hear everything that's been going on."

I take a huge swallow of icy water, which immediately gives me a headache. Just then, the waiter comes over and we place our order. When he leaves, she cross-examines me again. "I want to know how you're doing," she continues. I want to hear your thoughts, your disappointments, and your fears. I want to know it all. And I want to help you." She sits back. "After all, I know what it feels like."

"I don't want to talk about how I'm doing," I say. "Can you understand that?"

"Jessica, it's not healthy keeping your feelings inside! You'll make yourself sick."

"Let me decide what's right for me, okay?"

"Fine, fine," she says, hurt, as if I've attacked her. She nibbles on a fried shrimp, which she dips in mustard sauce after every bite. A couple across the aisle annoys me. They remind me of Joe and I when we first started dating years ago. They are sitting across from each other holding hands across the table. Every once in a while, he takes one of her palms and kisses it. He keeps getting up, kneeling across the table, and kissing her passionately. I watch them as if they can save my life. My mother follows my gaze. "You can tell they're happy," she says. "I remember feeling that way." She sighs. "God, it's been so long."

"Uh huh," I say. The waiter brings our food. My mother carefully approaches her food, sticking her fork into the center of each piece of chicken neatly and precisely, sipping her tea delicately, and wiping her mouth every so often on her napkin, which she places perfectly in her lap. I eat around the chicken and shove huge gobs of rice into my mouth, slovenly, my elbows on the table.

"You know, when I married your father I had a feeling it wouldn't work," she confides. "I remember thinking I wanted to run back down the other way and never look back as I walked down the aisle."

"So why didn't you?"

"I don't know. I was young. I was afraid he would get mad. I was just afraid of everything. I hadn't come into my own yet," she says.

My mother has been married three times. The first was to my father, James, in 1968. My mother was only eighteen. She became pregnant with me five years later and divorced him when I was a year old. I haven't seen or heard from him since.

The second one, Thomas, lasted the longest. He was a construction worker who would come home after work and expect food to be on the table. Then after my mother would serve him he would burp a million times and make her rub his feet. He used to yell at me if I got below a B on my report card. They were married for ten years. The last one, Charlie, ended last year. He was never home and I don't think my mother even knew him that well. Her marriages have all been failures, something she never hesitates to tell anyone who will listen.

Now she is searching for love. "Hey, you know what might get you back into the swing of things," she exclaims, after she has discreetly swallowed a bite of food and patted her mouth with the napkin. "This dating service I tried last week. I have two dates lined up and I simply can't wait! You never know, the love of your life could be right there waiting for you."

"I don't want to date," I say flatly. "I told you I don't want to talk about this! I don't want to talk about love. I don't want to talk about dating. I want nothing to do with sex or love. I just want to concentrate on other things."

I wish I could tell her how badly I mean it, but she wouldn't understand. My life is very centered and focused these days: sleep, wake up, eat, go to work, come home, eat, go to bed.

"I just wanted to help. That's all," she says.

We are practically done by now. She likes to linger after meals, pick her teeth with a toothpick, and analyze her feelings about recent events. I like to leave. I always want to leave wherever I am, as if my next destination would be any better. I check my watch.

"Look, I've got to run," I say.

"Where are you off to? I thought you weren't working today," she protests. "I thought we could walk around, go shopping, maybe take in a movie."

"I have to be somewhere."

"Where? We never see each other," she pouts.

I'm angry, irritated, and full—not a good combination. "Since when do you want to be my best friend?" I say, before I can stop myself. "I'm divorced, so now we can understand each other?" She reels back as though I've hit her. I feel mean, and then feel guilty for feeling that way. Joe used to say that I create my own guilt and blame others for it, while in reality it's something in me.

"I'm sorry you see it that way," she says, pissed. She whistles for the waiter in that way I despise and he hurriedly brings over the check, like he's her personal slave. People always listen to her. She charges the meal and signs her name on the receipt as if she's signing some important document. The whole time she ignores me. We stand up to leave at the same time. Silently, we walk out to the street. It's raining now and I wish I had brought a jacket. She sees me shivering.

"Jessica, for someone who is a grown woman, you certainly don't know how to take care of yourself. Always bring a sweater. That's my number one rule."

I always feel like a child around her. She takes off her long mauve jacket and hands it to me.

"Put it on."

"But now you're freezing."

"You're my child. Put it on," she commands. I obey. It drapes over me like a second skin, a perfect fit. We walk to our cars and she watches me get in. Hair soaking, she leans in my open window. "Next Thursday?" she asks. Because I want her to leave and get into her car, I say, "Okay. Next week."

"Same place?" she asks.

"Fine." I start the car and she backs away from the window.

"Good," she mouths, and waves enthusiastically. I drive away wondering what I've gotten myself into.

◄ ►

Saturday night: Joe calls. "Stop harassing me," he commands.

"I'm not harassing you." I turn down the volume on the television.

"I know it was you who called and hung up on my machine—nine times! Why don't you just leave a message, come out with what you want to say? Jesus Christ. We're not in high school, Jessica." I hear the exasperation in his voice and want to run from it.

"It wasn't me," I lie. I just can't help tracking his every move. Wondering where he is, what he's doing, who he's with. I feel pathetic and my own behavior makes me want to crawl under a rock. I just don't know how to deal with this. It's too big.

"I know you're lying," he says. "You've got to grow up. We're *through*. Get it in your head." He hangs up loudly. I feel crushed and more awake than I have been in a long time. I turn the television off and lay in the dark, a hopeless case.

◄ ►

The night before the second Thursday, I awaken from a dream in which my father is trying to get me to go on a trip with him. I agree, surprised and happy that he asked me. It doesn't occur to me that I've never seen him in my life. I just know him.

We decide to go on one of those bus trips to see the country, the kind where you pay a flat rate and don't have to worry about driving. It has been only half an hour on the bus when he suddenly starts to get panicky. "Wait, I don't want to be here," he says. He turns to the bus driver. "Stop the bus," he demands. The driver stops and my father gets out. He starts to walk down the road.

I run after him. "Wait! Wait for me!" I feel like my world is collapsing.

"You'll be happier somewhere else," he says. "Go back to your life."

I cry and fall on the ground, sobbing for what seems like hours, watching him walk away. He is how I always imagined he would look: tall, with brown hair, blue eyes— the perfect father. He keeps walking away and I keep crying and when I wake up I have a crick in my neck from sleeping wrong. I pace around my bedroom, dizzy and sick, trying to analyze what the dream meant so I can find some peace.

I realize suddenly that I miss something that I never had in the first place. The need is so great that my chest seems to rip open, and I panic—how could I have not cared about even trying to find him over the years? What if he is the answer? Maybe I am screwed up with men because I never had a real father.

I pick up the phone to call my mother.

◄ ►

We meet again; this time, I find her first. She looks beautiful as usual, wearing jeans and a crisp white blouse with the sleeves rolled up. I have actually taken some time with my appearance and feel somewhat confident in my summer dress, which I got on sale at Macy's. I want to appear cool and collected, in charge of my own life.

"You don't look like the person who called me this morning," she says, as the same hostess takes us back to our table. "You seem more put together."

"I feel a little better," I admit.

"Good. I was worried."

We both order the same thing as last time and the waiter smiles approvingly. I sip my water, which is ice cold again—too much for a painfully cold winter afternoon. "It's like they freeze this stuff or something," I say, shivering.

She takes a sip of her own and shudders. "God, it's probably because if it wasn't this cold people would just realize it was crappy New York City tap water and they wouldn't come back," she says, running her hands through her hair. "So, you had a dream about your father?"

The way she says it, so casual, makes me feel kind of

stupid. "Well, yeah," I tell her.

"Was it bad? You wouldn't tell me on the phone, which I didn't understand."

"I wanted to see you in person."

"Well, I always have time for you," she says, squeezing my hand over the shrimp and mustard sauce. That's a lie, and the fact that she doesn't realize this makes me a little angry. But I brush it off so I can talk to her rationally, without there being any hard feelings in the way. I've learned over the years how to deal with her in the same way I deal with an obnoxious boss.

I describe the dream and she sits back, sighing. "Sounds like something he would do," she says bitterly. "Just leave and never come back, forget about anyone and anything that ever meant something to him."

"I don't understand it," I say. "There must be a reason for him to act that way. No sane person would just ditch his family."

"He wasn't sane."

"Whatever," I sigh.

"So, what, are you saying you want to find him?"

The minute she says it, it hits me: I have a yearning to meet my father. I am tired of focusing on Joe and I am sick of my mother being my only parent. "Yes," I tell her.

"For God's sakes, he doesn't care!" she says, raising her voice, her face turning crimson. "You think he wants to see you? You'd think that if he cared he would have found you by now. You're twenty-five, Jessica, and your father doesn't give a *shit* about you." She takes out a cigarette, which I haven't seen her do in years. "I thought we were going to talk about your divorce, not this *horseshit.*"

I'm reeling from the fact that my mother swore and also from her unexpected reaction. I have never seen her so upset, not even after her second husband left her. I suddenly feel tired.

"But he's my father. I have a right," I say weakly.

"So go find him." She shoos her arm at me. "Have fun."

I'm slowly growing mad. I know somewhere inside that I really won't find him. It's the thought that I could that intrigues me. And for some reason I feel like he and Joe are somehow twisted together, that my feelings for both of them are sick and unresolved. I wish my mother could make sense of me. I wish I could make sense of myself.

"Mom..."

"I don't want to talk about him anymore!" she interrupts, taking another drag from her cigarette.

"But I was just trying to express my feelings. You said you wanted to hear about them."

"There are some things I just don't want to talk about," she says, "And James is one of them."

So for the rest of the lunch we talk about nothing, just everyday stuff, like her job and the somewhat famous celebrity I'm interviewing next week for the magazine. It was an assignment I got right before the divorce became final four months ago. We've always been good at talking about superficial things and never getting to what's really there, lying underneath the flesh. When we go to leave, she hugs me. "Stay well. I love you. See you next week."

◄ ►

The third Thursday.

My mother calls me at noon. I am in bed with the covers over my head, happy because I borrowed some Xanex from a friend and am finally feeling no anxiety. I drift in and out of warm sleep.

"Where are you?" she says loudly in the phone, the sounds of the street behind her. "I'm waiting at the restaurant."

"In bed." I bring the phone with me inside the covers and hold it away from my ear a little to avoid the annoying shrillness of her voice.

"Are you sick?" she asks, concerned.

"Kind of."

"What's kind of? You're either sick or not."

"I just feel strange," I say.

"Have you eaten?"

The last time I ate was yesterday morning. "Not recently," I answer, not caring how it sounds, not caring about anything.

"You need to eat, Jessica. You either come over here or

I'm bringing something to your apartment. Now come on!"

"Just bring me something, then," I mumble, feeling my voice drifting off, finding the comfort of sleep again. The next thing I know, my mother has barged in with her key and is standing over my bed, smelling like cool air and lipstick. She throws off the covers. "Jessica, get up!" she says.

I realize I am still holding the dead phone. I peek over at the clock—1:15. It has been over an hour. I wonder where she has been all this time. She is holding a bag with the name of the Chinese restaurant on it. My apartment begins to smell like garlic. I have been dreaming about sex, remembering how it feels, wondering if I will ever feel it again. I realize where I am and start to cry. "Oh, God," I groan. She is just staring at me. I wish she would come over and hug me but she doesn't. Instead, she goes into the kitchen and puts the food on plates. I have a feeling she thinks I am being melodramatic.

"You must eat," she says, handing me a bowl of rice and vegetables. "Just try."

I feel nauseous. "I can't."

"You can and will."

I am suddenly infuriated. "Don't play mother with me. You can't just be one when you feel like it."

She looks taken aback. "What, is this about your father?" she asks, gesturing to the room. "All this animosity toward me, toward your life? Look at you. It's past noon on a weekday and you're in your pajamas. Tell me what's wrong. I want to know."

"It's obvious what's wrong, mother! I have just gone through a fucking divorce. I am miserable," I spit out. "So excuse me if I don't feel like socializing right now. Please, just get out of here and leave me alone!" I turn over, my back to her.

"Fine." She gets her purse and opens the front door. She turns around and looks at me. "Just remember to eat." Then she slams the door behind her. I look at the food and want to vomit.

◄ ►

I spend the next few weeks in bed, only emerging to write articles for the magazine or go on the computer. I call Joe's machine a total of fifty times, hanging up before he can say hello. My mother calls every Thursday morning, asking me to meet her at the Chinese restaurant for lunch, but each week I refuse, telling her I'm tied up with work. I know she knows that there is something wrong. It is on the seventh Thursday that the shit hits the fan.

She calls me Wednesday night and pleads with me to meet her. "Do it for me," she barrages. "I want to tell you something."

"So tell me now," I say tiredly.

"I want to see you in person," she explains. "Okay? Please. It would mean so much to me."

I am sprawled out on my bed with books all around. They are all about how to find someone. I went on the

Internet and ordered everything about starting a search to locate a long lost loved one. Although he was never a loved one because I never knew him, but still ... I would never in a million years tell her I was looking. "Fine," I give in. "I'll meet you at the usual time."

"Yay!" she exclaims, like a little kid. I wonder what she is up to. "See you tomorrow, then."

"Okay."

There is a bald man wearing a non-descript pea green suit sitting next to her when I get there. I'm late because I slept through the alarm. She beams at me when I walk over to them. The man has his arm draped over her shoulders possessively.

"Jessica!" she exclaims, as if she didn't know I was going to be there. She stands up and gives me a hug.

The man says, "Hi. I'm Jerome." He holds out his hand, which I shake. It is as dry as sandpaper. My mother sits down next to him, and I sit across from them. I suddenly notice her ring. "I wanted the two of you to meet," she says. "Jessica, Jerome and I are getting married!"

I reel back. "*What?*"

She looks uncomfortable. "Umm. I know this is sudden, but I have been trying to get you to meet him for weeks. You've just been busy." She turns to him and kisses his cheek lightly. "We met about a month ago, and it was love at first sight."

He nuzzles her cheek with his nose. "Yeah." They giggle.

"Mother, are you crazy?" I hiss, grabbing her arm across the table. "Are you nuts?" She pulls angrily away. Jerome looks shocked and then embarrassed. I feel like telling him it isn't his fault, but I can't even look at him. I stand up to go, push my menu on the seat, and knock my water over.

"What on earth?" she exclaims, holding back her voice. I can tell she doesn't want to yell in front of Jerome.

"How can you make this mistake again?" I turn to Jerome. "Did she tell you that she has been married three times? One was to my father but obviously that didn't work out. She has a pretty shitty track record with marriages and men."

My mother sinks into her seat. "Jessica..."

People are starting to stare. I just can't take it anymore. I can't deal with her, with her fakeness and her problems and her need to be loved. "I know all about it," Jerome says quietly.

He dangles his arm over her shoulders. She sits there, slumped over, staring out at me from under her bangs, not speaking. For some reason she has become a mute. I have never felt so angry with someone for being so stupid— except for myself, like when I call Joe and hang up. The parallels between us are enormous. I hate the fact that I am becoming her.

I shake my head, put on my coat, and leave. They don't stop me. The friendly Asian hostess smiles at me, but

I don't smile back. I walk right out into the rain. Neither Jerome nor my mother comes after me, but I didn't expect it. I know that this is the last Thursday, partly because now Jerome is in the picture and partly because I have disgraced her. I am her life's biggest disappointment.

I get in my car and drive away, back home to my apartment. I can't wait to crawl into bed.

◄ ►

Two days later, as I am on my way back from a walk, I see Joe standing in front of my building with his dog. As if he senses my presence, he turns in my direction, sees me, and gives a feeble wave. Before I can stop myself, I wave back, and then he walks over to me. He looks horrible. He needs a shave, and his pants hang loosely below his hips.

"What are you doing here?" I ask, clutching my coat around me, using my free hand to pet Dudley. He used to be our dog but Joe got him in a custody battle.

"I just wanted to see how you were doing," he mumbles, staring at the ground. The he looks up and stares at me piercingly. "How *are* you doing?"

Dudley nuzzles my leg and I bury my hand in his wet, damp fur.

"I'm fine," I say. "Doing well, actually."

"You don't seem well. You look thin."

"So do you."

There is a brief silence, and then he blurts, "I miss you."

I take Dudley's leash. "Let's get out of the rain," I say.

He touches my shoulder, his hand lingering a bit. The heat makes my body flush.

"Just follow me," I say briskly. "It's freezing."

◄►

One more lunch with my mother—this time, it is on a Saturday.

The lunch happens by accident. We both are shopping at Macy's at the same time. I literally bump into her. "Oh, excuse me," she says politely, and then realizes it is me. "Jessica!" she exclaims.

"Mom!" We are long lost friends reunited.

After we get the initial friendliness out of the way, we just stare at each other for a brief second. I'm surprised at how I can know someone else's features so well, even after a long separation. It has been about four months since the episode in the restaurant. "So, did you and Jerome get married?" I ask tentatively.

"Just last month." She shows me her diamond ring. I feel an immediate pain in my stomach. I think of the three just like it in her dresser drawer, buried underneath mounds of tissue paper. "We drove upstate and found this wonderful little chapel. Then we honeymooned in Key West. I just got back a few days ago." She examines me. "You look different."

I avoid her question.

"You want to grab a bite?" I want desperately for her to say yes. Somewhere in me there is such a desire to please her that it suffocates me.

"Of course."

"But not Chinese. I just had it last night."

"Hey, I know," she says, gathering her bags together. "Why don't we just go grab a hamburger?" She is wearing a blue scarf that makes her eyes stand out.

I follow her lead and we walk to a fast food place. Her complexion looks dour in the fake lighting. We order the same thing and take our plastic trays over to the table. She unwraps the yellow packaging off her hamburger with concentration; I rip mine off. She folds hers and places it neatly next to the tray; I crumple mine in my hand and toss it near the napkin tray. Should I tell her I am back with Joe? I wonder.

"So what did you buy?" I say, keeping the topic light, eating a fry.

"Oh, just some blouses and a couple of skirts for the fall," she says. "I looked at all of my clothes and thought, time for a change! I love autumn, don't you?"

"Sure." My mouth is full. It is as if no time has passed. That's how it is with my mother.

"Jerome looks so good in the season's colors. He looks spectacular in green and burnt orange," she adds. At the mention of his name, I cringe. She notices and says quietly, "Well, he is my husband, you know. I can talk about him."

"I'm not saying you can't. Look, Mom, I'm sorry for the way I acted the last time we saw each other. I was in a different place then. You do what you want with your life. I want you to be happy. I was just concerned."

"And I've been concerned about you. I haven't heard from my own daughter in four months. How do you think that makes me feel?" She sighs. "I mean, I know the phone works both ways, but I never know what mood you'll be in."

"Things are going fine," I begin slowly. "I've been doing a lot of writing."

She raises her eyebrow comically. "Dating anyone?"

I suck in my breath involuntarily. "Actually … Joe and I are back together."

"What?" She drops her hamburger. "Are you serious?"

I nod. "Yeah." It's suddenly amusing to me that all of our dramas occur in restaurants. "Right after that day in the restaurant, I walked back home and there he was, standing across the street from my apartment with Dudley."

"Huh," she says. "How do you feel?"

I don't know, but I tell her, "Really great."

She beams and sits back. "So now we are both in relationships."

This is what she wants: Both mother and daughter are complete because they have men. Therefore, their relationship is solid. So I say, "Yeah, mom, we certainly are."

For the rest of the day we are best friends. We finish shopping, and then we see a movie. We eat dinner together and then we walk around the city, window-shopping. For the first time in a long while I feel totally connected to my mother.

As for my father, I never find him. Several months after the Saturday lunch with my mother, I am walking in the park with Dudley and think I see him. There is a man sitting by the pond and he looks exactly like me. He is wearing brown corduroy pants and a green shirt, the top button unbuttoned. It is a summer day and still light outside, even though it is dinnertime.

I walk near him and watch from afar. He is sketching something on a clipboard. I walk a little closer and see he is sketching a lily pad. Every once and awhile, he holds the pen between his lips in concentration just like I do. He appears to be in his early fifties. My heart jumps to my mouth and I start to shake, but I can't speak. For some reason, he senses someone is near him, looks around, and smiles when he sees it is me.

"Can I help you with anything?" he asks. "You look lost."

I say, "Oh, no thanks. I thought you were someone else."

He smiles a brilliant smile. "I'm sorry I'm not," he says. "Good luck finding whoever you were looking for."

"Thanks." I smile politely though I feel myself sinking.

I take Dudley home, where Joe is waiting for us. I never look back at the man; my feet just take me home.

Have You Seen My Mother, Delilah Bendin?

CURTIS SMITH

i look at my mother Delilah now and I know she's dying, that the cancer cells are multiplying in her withered body, unseen, like spawning fish beneath the river's flow. I think that's part of the reason she's acting so strange, not that the cancer has affected her brain, just her thinking. It's not hard to understand. Anyone who knows there's a detour ahead will map out a new route. It only makes sense.

She says she won't go to the oncology lab at Country General anymore either. "For the last months of their lives, I visited too many people to count in that damn hospital," she rattled harshly as I drove her home from her last chemo session, "and I know there's nothing I'm more dead set against than waiting to die in a bed that's not my own with tubes bringing my food in and taking my shit out."

Naomi

Naomi, my older sister, lives in a Streamline trailer about a quarter-mile from the house where we grew up. Weeds and wildflowers try to reclaim the trailer each summer, but

Delilah sickles them down in the afternoon heat, cursing and sweating, the honeyed scent of alfalfa drifting through the curls of her unkempt hair. When her sister Ruth and my uncle Eli died in a car accident on their way to Florida two winters back, something snapped in Delilah, a filament of faith or fair play that had been strained since the day my father keeled over from a heart attack, and now I think my mother actually welcomes her illness as a way to vindicate her darker beliefs. When I take Delilah to the doctor, I secretly spy on her over the top of glossy magazines, and I'll think how hard it must be to grow old, to tie one's dreams to something as fragile as human flesh. Here is a woman who grew up before they ran electric lines through the county, and I can't begin to comprehend how odd this world must seem to her now, the landscape of her youth paved over by moon shots and cable TV and microwave ovens.

Delilah's moods have taken their toll on Naomi. Although she's never said it, Naomi hasn't forgiven me for moving into town. Her exasperated phone calls have grown more frequent, and the strain of having to deal with Delilah on a daily basis is starting to show in the crow's feet that frame my sister's once youthful eyes. The most recent call concerned the mysterious disappearance of Mr. Mitchelson's bad tempered Doberman. Naomi swears Delilah shot and buried it in the secret hours of a moonless night. Says she saw the freshly dug grave behind Delilah's garage, but to tell the truth, I can't say I blame Delilah, the way that snarling beast was always treeing her cats and rooting through her garbage.

Naomi also frets about Delilah's obsession with flea markets and auctions. "Junk. That's all she buys. Fifty-year-old junk," Naomi complains, chain-smoking Newports and looking a little more like Delilah every day. "I just don't understand it."

I rent a two bedroom apartment over my place of employment, Ted's Diner. I've offered to have Delilah come live with me, but she'll have no part of it. Someday she'll probably have to, but for now I'm glad she's keeping our old house. Returning home, even when Delilah is in one of her moods, is so comforting, like wrapping myself in Grandma's patchwork quilt on a cold January morning when it seems winter just might go on forever. Naomi's a sweetheart, and I'm sure she'd offer to have Delilah move in with her too—that is if Delilah didn't already own the trailer and the land it sits on.

A Call

It was the week before Thanksgiving, and the breakfast rush was on at Ted's. A numbing north wind blew, winter cold a month too soon. Coffee smells twined around raw noses and earlobes. Naomi's phone call came as I balanced two orders on my right arm.

"Eden?"

"Hey, Naomi," I said, "is this important? We're really busy."

"It's Delilah."

"Is she OK?" I stammered. A side dish of scrapple slipped from my hand and hit the floor, shattering into a dozen spinning pieces. I had long been braced for the phone call that carried the news of Delilah's death, but I'd always envisioned it coming in the middle of the night, my head cloudy with sleep and my feet anchored in a cold sweat upon the tiled kitchen floor of my apartment.

"She's fine, the bitch, but she's stolen my car."

"What?" I half-laughed. Delilah hadn't driven since the big accident down on the square three years before. "Where do you think she's gone?"

"Out to some damn auction across the river. That's all she talked about this morning. When I said I wouldn't take her, she must've lifted my keys." She breathed hard through clenched teeth. "Damn her anyway."

"You sit tight and tell me where this place is."

"About a half-mile across the river. Just off the Brownsville exit." Her voice trailed as she lit up a cigarette. "Eden," she exhaled, "I snuck into her attic yesterday and you know what I found? More boxes and crates of knick-knacks and plain old shit that she's been hauling away from these damn auctions. And when I asked her about it, she nearly bit my head off."

"Don't worry," I said. "I'll head right out after my shift.

I was planning on driving out there anyway and checking out the new mall over in Clarkstown."

Her tone mellowed. "It's not the car I'm worried about."

"I understand, dear. We're both worried."

"I honestly don't know what to do anymore, Eden. I swear she's impossible."

"I know," I said. "I know."

Two Bedrooms

Main Street here in town is about a mile and a half long. There's the courthouse and post office on the square. There's a bank, a movie house, Ted's Diner, a sleepy array of apartments and shops. The mill and the incinerator on the north end. On the south end, a candy factory that sugar coats the whole borough when the winds come in off the fields. I moved here in an attempt to make a life of my own, but whether or not I've succeeded is a matter of debate.

At night, exhausted from my too frequent double shifts, I shower off the day and sit up in bed, listening to the street noises that drift up to my window of throaty engines and kids with nothing better to do than stand on the square. I watch TV or read the books I've checked out of the library, and when I grow too weary to keep my eyes open, I turn out the nightstand light, and in the darkness, I wonder if Delilah is asleep in her walnut sleigh bed. I think of her alone in the wintry, blue chrome glow that seeps through her windowpane. I think of her alone in this world, without Naomi or myself to indulge her, without the memories of giving birth, without the shoebox of faded snapshots she hides beneath her bed. I picture her sleeping alone for the past eighteen years, and I wonder if she still keeps my father's shirts in the back of her closet, or if she turns half-asleep in the night to touch his warm shoulders.

Old Things

I parked with the other cars in a cut wheat field. The littered stalks rustled crisp and hollow beneath my boots. Ahead, I saw the brownstone farmhouse, looking stripped and bare with its doors and windows flung open. Sitting all hollowed out in the cold air, it reminded me of the gutted, dull-eyed deer my father used to string up from our backyard elm.

I walked over the trampled grass of the courtyard, through a path of kitchen tables and worn furniture. There was that farm smell, dung and hides and broken earth, but no animal sounds since the livestock had already been sold. Charcoal clouds hung over men and women bundled up against the cold as they strolled through the grounds with hypnotic half steps. They paused at certain items—a glittering cut glass bowl here, a nicked footstool there—stroked them with gloved hands, hoisted them for inspection, and moved on. A pair of shoes grabbed my attention. Red satin pumps stained with grime, the material torn around the toes and heels. I picked them up and wondered how long it had been since they were worn, whether they were bought new for a wedding or a formal and how long they had been forgotten.

"Hey, Eden."

I turned and saw a thin man with hollowed cheeks. He smiled politely. Leathered wrinkles rippled through his face and elevated the red baseball cap on his head.

"Hi," I said. I had seen him at the diner, but I couldn't recall his name. "Been here long?"

"About an hour."

"Have you seen my mother, Delilah Bendin?"

"Wouldn't be a sale without her." He pointed toward the farmhouse. "She's right up there."

I spotted her on the porch, squeaking along in rubber overshoes. I could hear her talking to herself, cursing out loud and taking inventory as her bony hands sifted through the contents of the boxes at her feet. Her head shifted deliberately from the absurdly lavish white fur collar of her parka. Coarse strands of salt and pepper hair dangled like disconnected wires from either side of her checkered hunting cap. She was, in the succinct phrasing of her late sister Ruth, "a sight."

"Delilah," I called as I made my way toward her.

She looked up. Her green eyes burned into mine. "What the hell are you doing here?"

"What do you think I'm doing? Naomi says you stole her car. You're lucky she hasn't called the police."

"Screw her." She spat and turned her attention back to the box. A cigarette dangled from the shriveled corner of her mouth. "Only crime around here is that a grown woman who lives off the generosity of her mother can't lift her ass off the couch to drive her somewhere she wants to go."

"Delilah," I said, "you at least should've asked before taking her car."

"Why? She only would've said no." Her eyes passed over me. "You going to stay?"

I said nothing.

"You're not going to drag me back to that ungrateful sister of yours, are you?"

"Naomi's worried about you."

"Bullshit!" she snapped. She stamped her feet on the rotting floorboards to emphasize her passion. "Bullshit! Bullshit! Bullshit!" She halted, gasping for air. "Only thing she's worried about is me pissing away all the inheritance she figures she's got coming!"

Heads turned our way. "Come on," I said gently. I slipped my hand over hers. How frail it seemed! Her palm as thin as a child's. "I promise I'll take you to an auction this Saturday. I've got the whole day off."

"You promise?"

"Promise," I answered, crossing my heart.

A steady wind blew against our backs as we walked through the cut wheat field to our cars. Enveloped in the wind were the first crystallized twinges of winter ice; they caressed my exposed neck, making everything around me seem new and pure.

"Are you sure you're OK to drive?" I asked as she started Naomi's car.

She gunned the engine hard. "Been driving longer than you and your sister put together. Don't need any pointers now."

"OK. You follow me close. I'm going to stop by that new mall in Clarkstown on the way home."

"Mall?" she sneered, scrunching her face like a white prune. "There's nothing but shit in malls."

A Story

Delilah insisted the reason she ran Naomi's car into the first rows of a wheat field along State Road was because the brakes had failed. "Your sister never could take care of anything," she said as she settled into my front seat. "That damn thing is falling apart. It's an accident waiting to happen. If I didn't know better, I'd swear she was trying to kill me."

I started my car and pulled back onto the road. "Naomi didn't ask you to take her car."

"There you go! Taking Naomi's side again."

"What's more, you can barely see over the steering wheel."

Our words rattled off the plastic and glass of the interior. There was no way for them to escape, and they piled deep between us.

"How am I supposed to drive a shit bucket like that?" she barked. "Damn thing's out of alignment."

"I thought you said the brakes went."

She rooted through her purse and retrieved a cigarette.

"Do you have to smoke?" I asked.

"Piss off," she said. The cigarette twitched between her tobacco-stained fingers. She lit a match and cupped her hands. The butterfly seams of wrinkles stitched beneath her eyes shone in a golden moment. She exhaled. "Don't forget who taught you how to drive."

"I know, Delilah."

"And don't forget who bailed your sixteen-year-old ass out after you rear-ended the mayor's car."

"I know. You were always good to us." Smoke clouds began to form along the windshield. "Could you at least crack the window? Just to let some of the smoke out?" With a dramatic sigh, she rolled down her window a half-inch. "I swear I don't know who's worse. Your sister gives me the keys to a death trap, and you want to put me in a damn wind tunnel in the middle of winter."

Off in a field, a trash fire threw knotted black clouds into the sky. A pair of boys stood upwind from the orange flames, hurling tires and wood scraps into the blaze. The fire popped and convulsed as it consumed the debris.

Delilah leaned back and started to tell a story about a barn fire she'd seen as a little girl. She told of the crackling sounds of burning wood and the baying of trapped horses. She said once the roof caved in, it wasn't with a crash but with a gentle whoosh that was more like a fat man's sigh. She talked about the following morning, the buzzing of a thousand flies and the charred carcasses of animals half-buried in the mud.

Traffic snarled behind a tractor hauling a wide baler. I kept my eyes on the road, not wanting to rear-end another car as I had done ten years before. I glanced to my right as Delilah told the story of a barn burning in the blackness of night, but for a moment, she was gone, and I suddenly felt unsure of myself, my own substance, even the pedals beneath my feet.

New Things

At the mall, Delilah straggled behind me, mumbling obscenities beneath her breath. Already the salesgirls were busy setting up Christmas displays. Piles of cotton balls for snow. Blinking, candy-colored lights. At first, Delilah was confused, but I reassured her that Thanksgiving was next week, and no, she hadn't missed it.

"How much longer is this going to take?" she asked, her face focused around the straw of an orange drink she'd bought. "Can't stand these places with their hospital stink, rushing us through holidays that aren't even here yet."

"I want to look at a few shoe stores," I said. "We won't be but a half hour. Promise."

Delilah plunked herself down on a wooden bench that overlooked an artificial pond. Goldfish the size of ketchup bottles swam above a copper sea floor of pennies thrown in for wishes and good luck.

"I'm not moving," she declared. "My damn feet are killing me." She fumbled through her purse and lit a cigarette. "Good God, I'm tired."

Silently, I sat down next to her and pulled her ankles across my lap. I took off her shoes and began to rub her bony feet. Christmas carols played lightly over the speaker system. Seamless plate glass windows lined the front of the shoe store across from us, and they held our reflections, pale and faint. A pair of red high heels were displayed on a clear plastic stand. The shoes seemed to float in mid-air, ready to whisk away some lucky girl for a magical night of dancing and romance.

So Much Running and
Never Coming Home

LEONIE SHERMAN

I perfected the art of sulking during the turmoil of my teenage years. Quality time with my mother was limited to car rides. The beige vinyl seats in our boat of an Oldsmobile stuck to my bare thighs as we simmered through another unbearable humid summer afternoon.

Memories of my life before the age of fifteen were fragmented pieces of a kaleidoscope. Shake it and peer through the glass tunnel; beautiful images appear, but nothing you can grab a hold of. The slightest movement caused the whole thing to shimmer and change. Such were the scattered shells of my fifteen years and I did not know life could be any different.

The day my world burst open into shards of understanding, I rode in the back seat and silence hung in the air like stale smoke. My mother casually remarked on what a liar I had been as a young child.

Curiosity overcame cool. "What did I lie about?"

"Oh, you came home one time and told me Daddy had asked you to tickle his pickle. You refused to discuss it any further with me, so I suspected you were making it up, but

I called your father just to be sure."

My mother reached under the seat for an eight-track tape, her eyes focused on the road ahead. The rustle of her fingers searching among the debris on the floor filled the yawning chasm opened by her words.

Unleashed after restless years held captive on a tight chain, the sharp-toothed beast of my memories went for my throat, clawed at my tender flesh with tiny razor claws. These first memories of childhood trauma arrived like the monsoon after a long sultry May, bringing relief and untold damage in their wake. Memories of the annual summer visit with my father, being chased into the bedroom and snatched, a tub of Vaseline that sat on my bedside table for one long month of a summer visit. The featured presentation in this jumbled array of memory shards, each clear as cut glass, was a fifteen second clip in slow motion.

The scene began with a bathroom door, which creaked open from the inside. There stood my father, six feet two inches of pale mottled naked flesh still dripping from the shower. A cloud of warm moist air filtered out into the hallway. Steam filled the bathroom, shrouded the mirror, the scent of Aqua Gel hung suspended in the damp air. My father stood before the toilet, holding a foreign lump of flesh in one hand. Mute terror rooted me to the cracked linoleum floor. My father beckoned to me with his free hand and an oily voice oozed out of his parted lips.

"Do you want to touch it?"

A black curtain dropped abruptly on the scene and I was back in the broiling car. While I grappled with the fierce beast attempting to asphyxiate me, my mother hummed absentmindedly. The beginning strains of Dolly Parton crooning "Here He Comes Again" brought me back to the familiar Oldsmobile, my favorite song tumbling through the crackly speakers, my mother's distant singing.

But nothing was ever the same again.

Five years and a whole lifetime later I was working as a carpenter and apprenticing to an herbalist at a lesbian commune in Kentucky. Maples were shedding their splendid reds and oranges when I arrived at Spirral, and the bare skeletons of trees patiently awaiting spring gave me hope. I retreated to this women-only space with the intention of healing from the incestuous memories which continued to haunt me. The book *The Courage to Heal* was my roadmap and bible. My pursuit of healing had all the grace of a puppy first encountering snow, and was marked by the enthusiasm of a recently graduated college student set loose in the world.

Thank God for Ellen Bass and her book *The Courage to Heal*. The chapter "Families of Origin" occupied my thinking for weeks. I role-played different possibilities while putting up dry wall and drilling holes, mulled over scenarios while decocting blue vervain and melting beeswax to make comfrey-calendula salve until Jess, Kate, and Mary were so sick of my questions they urged me to just call my mom and see what happened.

I prepared carefully—I ate steamed roots and rice for dinner, lit a candle and sage in my room, held myself still in a circle of white light. Heat radiated from the pipe in the corner, the slick hardwood floor caressed the soft underside of my thighs and calves. I glanced down at my defense system. The book lay open to page 312: "Don't Buy the Bullshit." Despite the heading just opposite that page entitled "Don't Harbor Unrealistic Hopes" I did, but I realized that my high hopes were only the best possible outcome, not the most likely.

My mothers' sweet voice answered on the third ring, and I plunged ahead.

"Hey Mom, how are you?" Her answer to this question is always the same and she did not disappoint me this time.

"No, no sweetie, how are you?"

"I'm OK, but this whole winter has been pretty intense for me. I've been thinking a lot about Daddy, and you know, what it was like to visit him and stuff." Where was my carefully rehearsed spiel? I should have written a script. Silence drifted between us so I plunged ahead.

"Do you remember that time when I came home and told you he'd asked me to tickle his pickle? I don't remember telling you, but I do remember him asking me to touch his penis...." I took a deep breath. Words clotted in my throat, congealed like drying blood. Stars glittering beyond the double paned windows began to blink in my brain, the room spun.

"Mom," I said firmly, gripping the syllable like a life raft. "Daddy molested me when I was little."

My mother did not pause. She did not attack and she did not raise hackles in his defense. Her response was calm, cool, and collected, her voice smooth as silk. "Your father did not molest you. He thought I was a prude and was trying to introduce you to a different way of thinking about sex. He thought I was a frigid Catholic ex-nun and just didn't want you to grow up to be like me. He was only trying to show you that penises are normal..."

"Mom?" I interrupted the syllable now the cause of my drowning and the means to make it stop at the same time. "You aren't ready to talk about this. I have to go."

Even now, the endless echo of my mothers' words in my head makes me want to throw up.

◄ ►

"Leonie, what's bothering you? I can tell you've been struggling this whole visit." My mother sat me down in the kitchen, wooden chairs scraping against the tiled floor, and patted my hand gently. My first Christmas with the family in seven years had not been a rousing success by any standards. I had cried myself to sleep each night, face pressed into a pillow to muffle the sound, as I lay in helpless misery on our family couch.

An idyllic New England scene lay beyond my mother,

visible through the double paned glass of her kitchen windows. Snow graced the meadow and dusted the barren trees ringing the cornfield as daylight faded. The dishes from our Christmas feast lay glistening in the dish rack and leftover food was sealed in plastic and lain to rest in the refrigerator.

I composed my face before meeting my mothers' eyes. How did she know I was upset? Were my eyes bloodshot and puffy? Was my face streaked and swollen? Is there any way to conceal your emotions from the woman who held you in her belly for nine months, changed your diapers, and drove you to middle school dances?

There was no point in trying to hide my feelings from this woman sitting before me, gazing at me with such deep concern that the brittle wall around my heart cracked. I took a deep breath, checking my tone of voice, regulating my breath; "think Switzerland" I told myself firmly.

"Well, Mom, it bugs me to be sitting around the dinner table and you all start to talk about Daddy like he's a normal person. It upsets me that Meagan is going and hanging out with him in New York City, and they're not even related!" Easy, Tiger. Take another deep breath. Back off. Go slow.

"I know you all still have a relationship with him, but he molested me and I don't want to hear about him, it's too upsetting."

The ticking of the clock was my response. The refrigerator hummed, the clicking and drippings of a modern kitchen were amplified by the silence that followed. Congealed puddles of light held our faces in stark relief to the gloom swallowing the meadow and cornfield, the darkness held at bay by brittle glass and filament crackling with electricity.

A sigh issued from deep in my mother's chest. "Are we still talking about that?"

I couldn't take in the whole of my mother at that moment, I could only focus on the minute details which made up her face—her slightly bulbous nose, the broken ruddy capillaries on her left cheek, dainty earrings dangling from her delicate oyster ears, the ivory seashell embroidered on the front of her dress. Her mouth was moving and I strained to pick out words.

"I'm just concerned about you getting on with your life. When will you stop dragging this around?"

My lips formed words, released like bubbles from a scuba tank, floating in the thick air between us. "Mom, this is part of who I am. I'm tall and blonde, I have four brothers and one sister, my father molested me as a child. I can only come to peace with it. I can't will it away no matter how hard I try. It will help me come to peace with it if you can accept this difficult part of me."

My mother and I seemed to be following a script, and her next line was delivered flawlessly: "Leonie, your father would never do anything to hurt you. I understand you were traumatized by what he did, but can't you understand that he did not intend to hurt you, you just took it wrong?"

"Mom, we'll never know what he was thinking, why he did it..."

A rare interruption from my mother silenced me. "Let me tell you a story," she said quietly. "It's a story I told your father." She paused and drank deeply of her own breath. The rhythmic inhale and exhale was like surf pounding a beach, constantly reaching for shore and always hurled back with the force of its own longing.

"When I was three years old I opened the door on my stepfather while he was peeing. I'll never forget the sight of him, standing there with this, this, thing in his hand; I'd never seen a penis before. I stood staring in shock until he closed the door. When I met your father I was still scared of penises."

You can hear the cards falling down, the shuffle of falling leaves, the pieces of a puzzle forming themselves into a coherent picture with no help from human hands. My mother and I, two Leonies; so much in common, so much gone bad, so much running and never coming home.

"Your father didn't want you to grow up afraid of penises, the way I did. He was trying to give a gift to your husband, he was trying to help you, not hurt you."

Tears welled in my mother's eyes and began a slow journey tracing the contours of her face and slipping silently off her cheeks, creeping into a dark stain at the scalloped edge of her navy neckline. We hung there, suspended in time, resentment throbbing between us, our very identities at stake as we weighed out possible words and discarded them, watching silence blossom.

The wooden legs of my chair caught on tile and screeched a protest as I dragged my seat closer to hers and carefully removed her hand from where it lay limp on top of mine. She gazed at the table, tears continuing to slip down her cheeks, shame glowing in her face.

"Mom," I whispered, but she was beyond the realm of words. I took my place in the adult world when I reached up and placed my arms around her, murmuring soothing words as if to a child. "It's ok, go on, cry, you're safe here. The worst of it is over, you will be ok Mom, it's ok, it's ok, it's ok."

Sobs wracked her body, and we rested there, floating in this new sea of deepened understanding together, her body limp and weightless, arms flung limply around my neck as the waves gently guided us to shore.

When she was able to look up and blink back the tears, our eyes met and held each other for a long second before she spoke. Her face, whole and lovely once more, quivered with pride and relief, grief and compassion, a bewildering combination of powerful emotions. She pushed melancholy words free from her dry throat.

"Can't we just move on?"

◄ ►

As a child, I couldn't afford to upset my mother. She was an island of safety in the stormy sea of my violent unpredictable father. Never mind that my island sanctuary harbored dangerous wild animals or featured the occasional patch of vicious thorny plants and perilous steep cliffs. One could plunge to a sharp death with one misstep, but I learned to navigate carefully, even on the darkest of nights with no moon in the sky and the stars gone out. I treasured my island, which was, after all, my only home.

As a teenager, I savored rebellion. Now I am taking my place as an adult in the world. My relationship with my mother is marked by all the complexity, beauty, and flaws of an intricately woven rug. This rug is constantly being made; new patterns are added, nothing ever removed, and our lives blossom and take root around us. My mother and I are deep, loving friends, sharing what we can, making timid attempts to establish boundaries, laughing, crying, and exploring one another when we come together, writing letters, sending gifts, and speaking on the phone from our comfortable homes thousands of miles apart.

Our song is mid-composition, but the music is mesmerizing. We have not yet reached the tonic, that soothing note which ties it neatly into a bundle, but we raise our voices nonetheless, blending them together in the way only mothers and daughters can.

Pearls

MARSHA DUBROW

They're absolute death, pearls.
—Philip Roth, *The Counterlife*

maya stroked the Mailboxes Etc. package containing her mother's ashes. Her sister CeeCee began her third poem.

"My mother, Pearl, was a lustrous gem, and I, a ruby in her diadem."

Maya squelched a laugh that erupted like a belch. CeeCee shot a fierce look over her cat-eye reading glasses, but didn't miss a beat of her eulogy.

Rabbi Emeritus Lucien Bakst rose as quickly as his 86-year-old body allowed. "Thank you, Cee—"

"My next poem," she interrupted, "is 'Mother Love.'"

A few mourners tittered, and one man emitted a sigh like a death rattle.

"I'm gonna get piles again if we sit here much longer," Florence Melanowski confided to her husband Harry. She used a wilted, Porcelana-stained tissue to wipe sweat from her upper lip.

"Piles, epis," Harry snorted. "One more poem and half

of us'll die from heat stroke, the other half from plain stroke. Thank God we're at a cemetery."

CeeCee repeated the title and started anew.

"O Mother, my mother, I am a mother too.

"I, like you, am a mother of two—"

At least CeeCee's third and fourth poems were relevant, unlike her "Olympics Onomatopoeia" and "Summer's Scent" about "June's jubilee. Jujubes no longer jejune." Maya's jejunum roiled. In fairness, it was June.

Florence poked Maya, "So? Why aren't you up there? You're the writer in the family."

Maya whispered, "I didn't want to turn Mom's burial into my own performance. Like that saying about Teddy Roosevelt—'He had to be the corpse at every funeral and the bride at every wedding.'" Just like CeeCee and Pearl, Maya thought, while wishing she too had inherited that entitlement gene.

Even after death, Pearl Penina Glick had to have things her own way. It was rare for Jews to choose cremation. But she had said, "Why spend money on a coffin I'll never see?"

And combining the burial of her ashes with the unveiling of her tombstone a year after death, the *yahrzeit* ceremony. "My daughters should make two trips back to Houston for their dead mother? Visit while I'm alive, better."

Pearl had made a tape for her two-in-one ceremony, selecting her favorites from Verdi, Ponchielli, Donizetti,

Beiderbecke, Hank Ballard and the Midnighters, Elvis, and Mahalia Jackson. Only Mahalia could be heard clearly above the "whoosh whoosh" of mourners fanning themselves with the Kaddish prayer, printed in Hebrew and phonetics.

The fanning prompted CeeCee to read louder, but failed to ease the 97-degree heat or the 99 percent humidity.

"Whoever created an open-air synagogue chapel in Houston, this hellhole of humidity, must have been an anti-Semite," Maya thought. She surreptitiously blotted the crease in her prominent chin with a sodden linen handkerchief.

She had not sweat so much since her last "emergency" trip from home in Washington, DC to help her mother, whom she had called Penina, Pearl, Mom, or Mother, depending on Mrs. Glick's behavior of the moment.

Maya had rushed into her mother's apartment only to find her snacking on a cold mound of fettuccine Alfredo and lukewarm Diet Sprite, enhanced by sucks on the longest cigarette Maya had ever seen. Pearl had smoked heavily and defiantly for sixty of her seventy-four years.

An ash fell on pills assembled like a necklace around a Waterford tumbler of Ambassador scotch: an anti-depressant, a tranquilizer, thyroid supplement, beta-blocker, baby aspirin, and another tablet to lower her cholesterol level which hovered around 285, as did Pearl's weight.

"Well, Mom, the good news is, you aren't having a crisis.

Bad news is, you aren't having a crisis—but told me you were," Maya said.

"Just checking to see whether you'd come. CeeCee didn't."

"When, I mean if you have a real crisis, no one'll come."

Pearl gestured with her glass, making the ice tinkle at her daughter.

"Bills've been collecting since your last visit."

"Penina, you don't need a custodian."

Pearl wagged her head. Maya, as annoyed with herself as with the mockery, walked to the kitchen shelf where she had set up a financial filing system during her previous visit. Maya's attempts to take her mother through the instruction sheet and thirty labeled folders had failed as if payback for attempts to drill her younger daughter on addition-subtraction tables.

Months of unopened bills teetered atop the instruction sheet. Maya scooped up the envelopes like a deck of cards to be shuffled. "Your phone'll be cut off, electricity, Visa..."

"You'd never let that happen. CeeCee might. But, she knows you'll do it."

"I'm a daughter, not a fool." She heard echoes of Oliver Wendell Holmes's calling the First Amendment "the right of a fool to drool."

"Supercilious. Remember—I changed your drecky diapers."

"Knew you'd say that. But Mom, you changed much more than that."

Grasping to abort the ugliness, Maya switched to Pearl's introducing her to civil rights, anti-anti-Communism, jewelry through an add-a-pearl necklace, opera, and even rock 'n' roll.

"Remember that day you discovered Elvis? You zoomed out to buy 'That's All Right Mama' right before it got banned. Damn, you built the best collection of contraband rock."

Maya always invoked Elvis, the quintessential dividing line of the generation gap, to stop mother-daughter arguments when nothing else worked. Minutes passed in silence except for Pearl's inhalation and exhalation of smoke. Then Pearl commented, "I still have the condolence card you sent the day Elvis died."

"That's the nicest thing you ever told me."

Maya looked at her in hopes that a meeting of their eyes might solidify their rare meeting of minds. But Pearl was looking down, as if watching the Sun record go around and around at 45 revolutions per minute on their hi-fi.

Maya eased back into her point. "I won't keep coming back as a bill-payer. And you've got to accept that Dad's not coming back. Like I said after he died—you always wanted to handle the finances, and now's your chance. As for CeeCee, she doesn't come for real crises, much less faux crises."

"Some first-born she is."

"Tell her, not me."

"She won't take care of me while I'm alive; she sure as hell will after I'm dead. I made her the executrix of my will." Pearl smiled and jauntily flicked the ash off her cigarette.

"That's macabre—and malicious, against both of us. Co-executors. You've got to change it." Waving away curlicues of smoke, Maya scraped her chair closer to her mother.

"How do you want us to remember you? As the fantastic mother our friends wished were theirs? Or as the mother who manipulated us against each other until the day she died? Even after that? Your choice, Mom. Please, make it soon."

◄ ►

Throughout Pearl's "emergencies" for undiagnosed physical and psychological ailments—and before that, their father's two heart attacks—CeeCee had stayed home in Bethesda, Maryland.

When Maya had been accepted for a month's residency at a writers' colony, she negotiated an agreement with her sister to take care of everything their mother might need for that month. But CeeCee phoned Maya two weeks into her residency and said, "You've got to go to Houston. Mom's flipped out again."

"Cee, you promised. I took care of her for seven years since Dad died—you agreed, one month in exchange for seven years."

"Did not."

"Of course you did. Look, parents get sick—you phobic about it? For once, handle Mom like you promised."

"You're lying."

"You're betraying me."

"Oh, save your drama for whatever you're writing," CeeCee's tone rose to the timbre of fingernails scraping a blackboard. "Your mother's more important."

"But your suburban haven's more important than your mother or your sister."

Maya remained at the writers' colony and CeeCee remained at home. She imported Pearl to a locked ward at the National Institute of Mental Health in Bethesda.

At that point, CeeCee declared herself a writer. First, she crafted a political romance novel. Maya offered the title, *Fornigate*, as well as her own literary agent. After amassing rejection slips, CeeCee tried poetry. Her prime endeavor since then was writing poetry and hawking it with the determination of an Amway distributor.

In the year since their mother's death, CeeCee had sent Maya ten invitations to her poetry readings. But the only thing she wanted to receive from CeeCee, sole executor, was a check for Maya's tiny inheritance.

Each negotiation to release the sum, so minuscule Maya had termed it an "inheripittance," reminded her of earlier power struggles: CeeCee heaving Maya's baby carriage down a flight of stairs, with infant Maya inside; purloining Maya's add-a-pearl to add to her own as a double strand; luring away most but not all of Maya's boyfriends; refusing to drive Maya to ballet class until she whacked CeeCee's knee with a brass vase.

Maya savored that one, down to the black oxidation marks the metal vase left on her sister's left kneecap, and on her own right hand.

Each time Maya pressed for an installment of her funds, she could hear Penina clucking, "Oh, girls, why can't you get along," and chuckling at her legacy—both daughters competing over her dead body, and for what little she'd left behind.

The deterioration in the sisterly relationship saddened Maya. CeeCee was her only sibling, and Maya was losing her, although forfeiting her, not long after losing their mother. CeeCee was also the brightest, funniest person Maya knew, even having an anti-depressant effect—the only person Maya let in. During one of Maya's worst bouts, CeeCee dropped in when Maya was on her second mug of espresso.

"Black dog got you again?"

"It's that obvious?"

CeeCee shrugged, "I'm your sister." She walked past her to a picture window and yanked the cord on the blinds which screeched against each other. "Depressed people need light." She pulled up a second set of blinds, letting in what little sunlight filtered through Rock Creek Park.

"C'mon, time for acquisition therapy."

"You know I don't shop even when I'm not depressed. Besides, no money."

Maya pointed the way out with her coffee mug. A black drip soiled the scarlet mug emblazoned with LIFE in white letters—her last of many perks as Washington Correspondent before *Life* died. When her next two magazine clients folded, the losses depressed her as well as her bank account.

"Look, how can I put this—thanks, but let me alone."

"Let me help." CeeCee gave her a brittle embrace.

Partly resentful and partly thankful, Maya sighed, "You're the only one who can lift this anvil off my chest— by an ounce, for an hour."

◄ ►

How different that was from the last time CeeCee visited unexpectedly, on Maya's birthday six months after their mother died and six months before the burial.

At the door, CeeCee presented one scentless iris and one unaddressed envelope. Maya looked inside the envelope for the check promised before her birthday. Seeing none, she whined, "This is the third time you've broken your word."

"Did not."

"You know you did." Maya felt they had catapulted decades back to "Yes-you-did; no-I-didn't; you-did-too;

uh-uh; uh-huh."

CeeCee, sounding like she'd inhaled nitrous oxide, said, "You're lying."

"Oh? You're withholding my money."

"Sure, I'm a regular Social Security. I keep saying, you don't understand the legalities."

"I cover the Supreme Court but can't fathom a simple probate case? Already approved by the judge? No legalities left to understand."

"You're whacko."

"You're repetitive. But prove I'm crazy—fork over my inheritance."

"You are so ugly when you're angry. You're just a depressive I try to help."

"Help? Stop punishing me—all I ever did to you was be born!"

◄ ►

Rabbi Bakst finally recaptured the podium. "When Maya asked me to give the eulogy, I asked her to jot some notes to refresh my aging memory. Well, let me just say I chose to read what she wrote. You'll see why."

Maya glanced at CeeCee who looked abashed. Maya regretted the rabbi's compliment almost as much as she embraced it.

Rabbi Bakst read, "Mother left New York City in 1939 to marry Dad, Melton Glick, in Permian Basin, Texas. It seemed as romantic as *It Happened One Night* and other

Depression-era films. But soon, Mother felt that living in Texas, and briefly Pawhuska, Oklahoma, was more like *The Grapes of Wrath*."

Maya looked furtively at CeeCee who was nodding in agreement. Their eyes met but Maya turned away when the threat of tears stung her eyes and nose. One tear rolled down her sharp jaw line and six-inch-long neck both sisters had inherited. As the drop continued along the upsilon of her collarbone, she recalled her ballet teacher's instruction, "Hold your arms as if a pearl could roll down and not fall until reaching the tip of your middle finger."

The rabbi read, "When my high school boyfriend's mother entered our house on Willow Forest Road, she said, 'You can feel the love in this home.'

"One of Pearl's greatest loves was teaching, helping others find answers. Another love was helping women, minorities, and disabled individuals find jobs even before the 1964 Civil Rights Act. Despite all this, peace eluded Mother. May she now have found the 'answers' and the peace she sought."

◄►

Walking to the gravesite, Maya hugged more than carried the box of ashes. She stanched tears by telling Pearl, "Mailboxes Etc. should advertise its cremains mailing service. Profitable."

Since her mother's death, Maya had the chats she wished they could have had when Pearl was alive. "Well,

Penina, seventy of your friends came. If we're reincarnated, I want to return as your friend rather than your daughter."

She bent down at the gravesite and lifted the twisty-tied plastic bag of ashes out of its box. She set the box behind her and hoped it wouldn't blow away in the welcome breeze. Rabbi Bakst led the Kaddish, then nodded to her.

She kneeled close to the birdcage-sized grave, unwound the green twisty and began pouring ashes like detergent into sweaty laundry. But a gust blew the gray-white dust into her face. She choked and coughed, trying frantically to wipe the chalky powder from her eyes. Several mourners gasped, some looked away, and Florence held out a tissue.

As Maya rubbed at the ghostly smear, she could hear her mother saying, "Even this, the last thing you'll ever do with me, you can't do right. Just let your sister do it."

Maya leaned so close to the grave, she could smell its fecund black soil. Determined to inter her mother, she upended the bag and dumped the remains deep. She stared in disbelief at the pulverized eggshell-like ashes.

Then she crouched closer still, and whispered, "That's all right, Mama."

God Is in the Cracks

ROBERT SWARD

"Just a tiny crack separates this world
from the next, and you step over it
every day," he says.
"God is in the cracks."

Foot propped up, nurse hovering, phone ringing.
. "Relax and breathe from your heels," he says.
"That's breathing.
So, tell me, have you enrolled yet?"

"Enrolled?"

"In the Illinois College of Podiatry."

"Dad, I'm a novelist."

"Ha! Well, I'm a man of the lower extremities."

"Dad, I'm forty..."

"So what? I'm eighty. I knew you
before you began wearing shoes.
You're a podiatrist, goddamn it!"

"I'm sorry, Dad. I just don't have it in me."

"Too good for feet?" he asks.

"'I. Me. Mind:'

That's all I get from your writing.

Your words lack feet. Forget the mind," he says.

"Mind is all over the place. There's no support.

You want me to be proud of you? Be a foot man.

I'm telling you, feet have it all over the mind.

Arch supports. Now there's a subject for poetry.

Some day you'll write about arch supports."

"I'll try," I say.

"Here, son," he says, handing me my shoes,

"Try walking in these."

My Mother's Teeth

C. A. PECK

y mother had all her teeth removed when I was eight years old. She returned from the dentist and I was afraid to see her so I stayed outside, hiding. What wild imaginings this event must have stirred up in my mind. I finally mustered up the courage to enter our basement apartment, an underground cave where a standing adult looking out the window would be eye level with the grass or someone's feet. I don't remember how I stood, how I looked, or whether or not I was crying, but my mother, in her thick Scottish brogue told me that she was OK and not to worry. She must have seen terror in my eyes. She saw something that needed reassuring. It turned out that the dentist was removing her teeth in quadrants so in fact she still had three quarters of her teeth intact. It didn't matter. It was still shocking. Half of her mouth was filled with cotton batting and soaked with blood. If she was in pain she didn't say anything. She didn't complain. Life continued as usual. She worked the next day.

I asked her why she had to get her teeth out and she replied, "pyorrhea." I remember that word to this day and have always associated it with having children, because when I asked her where the pyorrhea came from she said,

"Having you and Bruce." Her tone was not accusatory, just matter of fact. I have never felt guilty. I believed that giving up your teeth for children was normal. I am not a mother and I still have all my teeth. Maybe subconsciously I never wanted to take the risk.

Looking back, some forty years later, I know that pyorrhea is an inflammatory condition of the gums causing the formation of pus, possible swelling and pain, and eventual loosening of the teeth involved. In other words, if the process goes unchecked your teeth fall out. The gums become rotten with infection and this eats the bones of your teeth. This event, also known as periodontal disease, may be caused by poor dental hygiene. My mother was born and raised in Scotland. I was born in and lived my first five years in Scotland. I know from personal experience that dental care was not a priority to the people of the United Kingdom just after the Second World War. One of my most vivid and lasting memories of living in Scotland is going to the dentist and having a tooth pulled without anesthesia. I have no idea why a baby tooth was being pulled out. Maybe I had pyorrhea from being born. My mother said she heard me screaming all the way up the street to where we lived. Why she wasn't with me I don't know. Those painful screams are still in my cells. The morning after this trauma, laying in a bed I shared with my mother and brother (my father was in Canada looking for work), I awoke to a blood-soaked pillowcase. Instead of being white, my pillow was fully crimson. Dentistry in Edinburgh in the 1950s was not cutting edge. After having been in Canada for a few years I visited the dentist and left with a diagnosis of thirteen cavities. It is obvious that dental hygiene was not a priority in my family.

In defense of my mother's theory linking pyorrhea and giving birth, periodontal disease can occur in the presence of good hygiene and without obvious cause. My brother and I may have stolen all my mother's calcium to make our own teeth and bones. Perhaps her immune system was depleted and imbalanced from the enormous stress of raising two children, making a new start in a new country, cleaning houses six days a week to make a living, and keeping an eye on a philandering husband. Who knows?

I only remember my mother's false teeth. I do not recall what her real teeth looked like. Even after peering intently at before-children photos I do not have a clear visual of those teeth. The pictures are old and sepia colored. There is one photo of her that is presently in a box somewhere. She was a batwoman in the WAF's taking care of the needs of British officers. Her teeth look just fine, but what captures my attention more than anything is her smile. I can't get past all that beaming to focus on her teeth. She tells me her teeth were beautiful. Maybe. She is a smoker and drinker of exceptionally strong black tea. They must have been beautiful and stained, unlike her false teeth, which, thanks to nightly soaks, are beautiful and shiny white. I will find that picture and examine it once again. I want to get a better idea of what she gave up for my brother and me. I shall ever be thankful for my mother's teeth.

Blind

CHERIE JONES

d idn't know I was invisible until I passed 106th and Bethel. Must have been. Invisible I mean. Walking along with my mother and she was spitting mean. And rushing me too. Which really pissed me off because I was sweating all over my cat suit and in parts I looked like I was bleeding. My mother was tripping on about me being suspended and all. "Don't think you going to spend the day running about with boys and doing GOD ONLY KNOWS. What you need is some good West Indian discipline. Bring you here for some opportunity and you don't even appreciate it."

Don't know why she bothered to bring me here in the first place. It's cold as ass in the winter, hotter than chili peppers in the summer, and a host of windy, rainy in-betweens. I got suspended for giving it good to Sasha-Marie up in the hallway at the high school. Just only managed to secure me a man after a whole three months and she come batting her breasts in his face trying to take him. Back home, all the girls know beforehand not to mess with me. So I didn't have to show nobody. Not my fault she brought me here.

Stuck me up in two little rooms over a corner store

owned by this yellow Indian lady with a bull's-eye in the middle of her forehead and rolls of belly coming out of the sides of her sari—Mrs. Laskhmi. Mrs. Laskhmi keep bringing us curry this, curry that on account of my mother having to feed me and work the double shift at the doctor's. Seem like she just be waiting behind her door for Ms. Marie to come out for the evening shift to appear with her bowls full of curry. Nasty yellow stuff in Tupperware bowls she always reminding us to bring back. And Ms. Marie. She keep taking the bowls and smiling ever so grateful saying the last curry whatever was oh so good and she will just be putting it back inside so I can warm it up before she has to hurry off. And then she shutting the door and throwing the stuff right in the bin. And I have to be the one to return Mrs. Laskhmi's stupid Tupperware. Well one day when she came, when Ms. Marie had the day and the evening shift, I just sat me down and ate me that whole bowl of curry. Why, I almost made myself sick with laughter thinking how Ms. Marie's face would look if she had seen me eating that curry. I washed the bowl before she even had to ask me. And I still laugh sometimes thinking that I ate it and she didn't know.

But anyhow, the point is that I had to show Sasha how we do it in St. Kitts. I think I made her swallow a good few of her teeth. Now she bound to think twice before she go messing with my man again. But now I'm suspended and Ms. Marie having fits like something terrible. She near wring the be-Jesus out of my shoulder when the principal called her. Come to find out that she had lost her job the same day. Doctor seeming too fresh for her. If she'd a let me I would have fixed him proper, doctor or no.

Anyways, so Ms. Marie been sniffing a job all this week and all this week I been having to walk up and down, in rain, sleet, and snow while she knock on doors begging for work. She saying seeing how it is in the real world will keep my behind in school and on the straight and narrow. Well, I plan to show her. Says if that don't do it, she will send me back to St. Kitts just as fast as day becomes night. I wouldn't mind no how. Except for Roger Sparrow.

Which brings me back to being invisible—106th and Bethel. Pulling a wedgie out and trying not to walk too close to Ms. Marie who puffing for a ten o'clock interview and wringing my shoulder something terrible. And there he was: Roger Sparrow coming out of the McDonald's with Ms. Swollen Jaw Sasha. And I am thinking, *Ain't I done told that bitch?* And Ms. Marie, stopping at the bus stop. And Roger Sparrow, he looking right at me—through me. Like I never even there. Even with my red spandex on and a three-inch black belt sharing my waist, in case he missed it in all the red.

And Ms. Marie done banned me from speaking to Roger Sparrow or Sasha Marie ever again. But he looking right at me like he wouldn't hear me even if I spoke to him. And then Ms. Sasha was showing him something on her jaw and God bless Marie, he kissed it for her. And I knew I had to be invisible 'cause the thrashing I gave that girl, she would have to be blind, deaf, and dumb to kiss my man right in front of my face like that.

And then the bus pulled up and Ms. Marie was yanking my shoulder again and my red wig was almost falling off. So I righted it. And 'fore I could say "God bless Moses" the bus was moving on and Roger and Sasha were strolling away. Arm in arm, just as comfy as could be. And all I am thinking is, *I must be invisible*. And I said, "Ms. Marie can you see me?" And then I was sorry because her face, under her best black hat with the yellow rosebuds, looked worse than the last hurricane that hit home two years back. "Don't you be trying no stupidness wid me gal. I will fix your ass proper. Ain't tekking no foolishness from you."

Long time now I been thinking of running. I was fixing to run with Roger but now I am thinking how can you run with someone who don't even see you. I was fixing to run with Roger because he was my man. Down under the bleachers after school these past two months he been showing me just how much man he was. And I let him. I used to make him sing to me while he did it. The manly part I wasn't too fussy about but for an American boy Roger could sing him some Bob Marley. Last Thursday it was "Waiting in Vain." And for a whole week last term it was "Buffalo Soldier". Just filling me up with all those songs. His notes stroking my ears, closing my eyelids,

149

heavy on my thighs. With those notes Roger don't have to kiss me or even hold me. Mostly he just kept his hands on the bleachers. For balance.

Anyway, that was why I chose him. For his songs. I had imagined him singing to me. All the way out of the school gate in winter when I had had my fill of this God-forsaken place. All the way down the avenue. All the way onto the bus. All the way to the bus station. Song after song. All the way to the airport, on to the plane. Back to St. Kitts. I know I can't stand to hear another Bob Marley song again. But that Sasha. God bless Moses if I don't get back in that school and fix her proper, and if she ever try to come in my face she going to have to swallow the few teeth I left her with.

"You can't even dress decent to come out," says Ms. Marie. We getting off the bus. She on my shoulder as usual. I would never tell Ms. Marie about Roger. She don't understand no songs that ain't church songs. And I guess it would be a sin for a man to sing those to her.

Another Indian lady answer the door. And Ms. Marie say she is Ms. Marie here about the baby-sitter position. The woman, she nod. But she don't open the door wide, she just looking at me through a crack. And I am fixing to tell her why she looking. And Ms. Marie say my relative from the island. And that just throw me 'cause God bless Moses I ain't no relative. I am her daughter. Even though I hate her. Even though I told Marie Herschelle that we just

150

friends. Even though I told Roger my mother was dead. I am her daughter.

But Ms. Marie she still talking, "Sick and didn't want to leave her at home. Plus she learning to get around for when she going to school." The Indian woman, she taking in my red cat suit and broad belt and my red boots with the baby-doll heels and the little daisies cut out in them. And my leg warmers and my denim jacket with the peace patches and my three-inch earrings, and my red lipstick, and my red wig that cost me $19.19. Which back home, by the time they add the tax and everything, would be a fortune. Back home I couldn't afford this hair. But with an allowance from Mr. Roger, I could.

Well I just take the woman in back. Old coolie chick. No spine left in her. Looking at me with her beady black eyes. Her greasy hair almost cover her face. Her hand taking the keys out the pocket of her housedress. It have pink ribbons round the pockets. Ms. Marie, she sit down after she take off her shoes and I just sit down. The apartment dark. It have heavy red curtains with gold thread. It have pictures of people with jade for eyes and six and seven hands and feet sitting cross-legged on the backs of elephants. It dark and red. The chairs red, big and deep. The carpet like blood running under Ms. Kernani bare yellow feet. It have plastic cover over everything. And I sit down in a red chair and feel at one with the wall: a kind of yellow but with the drapes pulled it look like orange. And the

Indian woman say, "Come Phagwan, come Phagwan." And Phagwan come out in the front room, still in his pajamas, holding a blanket and sucking it and looking at my red wig with his mother's beady black eyes.

"It hard," she saying to Ms. Marie, "running the household and caring for Phagwan. We have three other children."

And Ms. Marie saying, "Oh me dear, yes, I can understand. It difficult, yes?" And the Indian woman watching Phagwan watch me.

"You have experience?" Ms. Marie hand her all the papers that she keep in her purse. References. Health certificate.

"No Green Card?"

Ms. Marie barely shake her head. "Just a few years I here now. It not straighten out yet. But I work real hard!"

The woman ain't saying nothing. And Phagwan still swallowing up my hair with black beady eyes.

"Phagwan. Show the nice lady your hamster."

Phagwan race back in the doorway that bring him and come back out with the little rat. Ms. Marie never like rats. Ms. Marie fidgeting and the woman watching her. Phagwan approach with the thing prostrated by the scruff of its neck.

He put it on Ms. Marie lap and I see her swallow. Swallow. Swallow. "Good little hamster, you take good care of him Phagwan?" And her hand trembling and it still on her lap. It never even trying to reach the hamster.

The time back home when I thought I saw a rat in the kitchen and I shout "Rat!" and almost make Ms. Marie burn the bake she scream and run so hard and fast. That time Ms. Marie beat me around the house. And God bless Moses I swear she almost kill me.

But Ms. Marie just trembling looking at Phagwan's rat.

"Okay," say Ms. Karnani, "Take him back, Phagwan."

Phagwan retreat and return with the blanket.

"There were so many applicants," the woman say, putting on her spectacles to read Ms. Marie papers, "So many good people."

"I been doing this forever," say Ms. Marie. "I love children. That's the best qualification. When you really love children."

And she motioning to Phagwan to come, come sit on her lap while she talk to his mammy. Phagwan not coming.

"In and out of the house every hour since I put the ad in."

"All I do since I come here is care for children," say Ms. Marie, "and at home I took courses in it."

She produce the papers and Ms. Karnani put them on a side table, a stone elephant, holding up her tea, a wet cord and tag dripping green.

It was the last place Ms. Marie call before the phone got cut off. Things been hard since the doctors. Which is why I told her she could have left me at home anyways.

Can't call nobody nohow.

"So many good people," say Ms. Karnani.

Phagwan make up his mind and come and sit on Ms. Marie. Ms. Marie still her hands enough to hug him. Close enough for Ms. Karnani to see she mean it but not too close like she could give him any cold she bring with her from outside. She bounce him on her knee and her hat with the yellow rose buds drop off and onto Phagwan head. And he laugh and show her his missing front teeth. And Ms. Karnani laugh.

And I was invisible again.

Ms. Marie watch Phagwan turn the hat in his hand. The hat she keep under her bed in the blue box with the white tissue and the rose petals. She watch Phagwan spin it on his forefinger, watching the flower go dizzy and shed its petals. Ms. Marie watch them go flying over Ms. Karnani's head and land on the papers, catch on the stone eye of the elephant table, the floor. And Phagwan laughing. Laughing. Laughing. Smiling with Ms. Marie. But is not Ms. Marie. 'Cause nobody can play with Ms. Marie's hats. Far less mash up her flowers.

"Oh, Phagwan," say Ms. Karnani.

"Is alright," say Ms. Marie, "he just a little child. I know how they do. I been caring for them for years."

And just so Ms. Karnani make up her mind.

Now she talking money. Quiet-like. She understand about the Green Card. Saturday's too, 'cause is then she do the shopping.

And I crying because I know I loss my skin. My hands, my head. Even in red I can't be seen. Not by Roger and not by my mother.

At the bottom of the stoop of Ms. Karnani's building, after she has retrieved her petals and put on her shoes and rustled Phagwan's rat-like hair, Ms. Marie try to grab up my shoulder.

But I raise my fist to her and twist away and I dare her to try and touch me. And she frown at me. She shake her head. She start to walk. Talking about if I was back home in the island and which tamarind rod she would keep for me.

But I don't mind her. She not going trouble me again. Don't see why I was ever afraid of her in the first damn place. Is now I see she is just another woman. And God bless Moses. As woman she have to see me.

The Elephant in the Room

LAURA DAVIS

y mother and I are sitting across from each other on my living room couch. The springs are shot from children jumping on them, so we both sink down a little beyond the point where it's comfortable. The fabric on one of the arms is frayed. I am sure my mother notices, but she doesn't say anything. There is a tape recorder between us, and a microphone on a stand. My mother knows that I've been working on this book about reconciliation and I've invited her to tell our story from her point of view. I explain that I am going to talk and respond as an interviewer, rather than as a daughter. I assure her that if we need to talk things through, we can do so later.

I ask my mother to tell her story in the third person, as if she is talking about an imaginary daughter, rather than me, believing that might make things easier for both of us. When I am about to begin, I look up, sensing my mother's reluctance. "You've hurt me in print before," she says. "I want you to promise that you'll let me read everything you want to say about me."

"Okay, Mom," I tell her and I mean it. I don't want this interview—or what I write about her—to undermine the progress we've made toward reconciliation. I've grown to care deeply about how my mother feels, and I have learned painful lessons about the power of words, so I reassure my mother, "Yes, you can read it and if there are parts you don't like, we'll work it out together."

My mother hesitates and shifts uncomfortably on the couch. I sense her inward struggle. Part of her believes me, part of her is not so sure. Finally, she decides to trust me; I see the change in her eyes. Tentatively, and then with increasing candor, she starts telling our story from her point of view. "For a very long time, starting when she was a teenager, I felt like my daughter hated me and I really couldn't figure out why. I always saw myself as a loving mother.

"It was extremely painful for me because I was at a very vulnerable time in my life. I was trying to find my way on my own after my husband left me, I was worried about my son who was away at college experimenting with drugs. And the only person I was living with was this daughter who was angry with me all the time. There was nothing I could do to please her. I tried everything in my power to support her after her father left us. I hoped her anger was just teenage rebellion, her reaction to me as the custodial parent who tried to set the limits. But she just kept drifting farther and farther away from me—living her life in total opposition to how I hoped she would live. She turned down a scholarship to Wellesley. She became involved with a guru. She moved far away from me. But the worst part wasn't what she was doing; it was how much she distanced herself from me.

"As the years went by, we had less and less in common. There was less we could talk about, less that might bring us together. Things went from bad to worse. I just about accepted one decision of hers when I'd be confronted with another disappointment and then another and another. Then came the final blow. She called to tell me that my father had sexually abused her. When in my shock, I reacted to that—granted, not in the best way—she got mad and wouldn't talk to me.

"My daughter wrote a very popular book in which I felt personally attacked and humiliated. It put me in a position of being torn between my caring about her and my original family, and it almost destroyed me.

"After that blow, my daughter and I both made efforts to come together, but our lives had diverged so much that it was hard. There were so many things we couldn't talk about.

"At one point, I flew across the country to go to therapy with her, and I felt like she and the therapist ganged up against me. They expected me to grovel and say, 'I'm sorry, everything I did was wrong,' but I couldn't do that. Instead of making it better, therapy only made things worse.

"My daughter and I tried to talk a few other times, but we could never make any progress. Finally, we both came to the conclusion that these efforts to get validation from each other weren't going to work, so we decided to leave the unresolved stuff sitting there.

"We've never been able to talk about the force that drove us apart the most—the accusations of sexual abuse. I've had to accept that my relationship with my daughter cannot include her memories of my father."

My mother's voice is intense with feeling. She is reliving every bit of the pain. She turns to me, her eyes vulnerable and filled with tears. I hand her a tissue. Our hands touch and I take her hand in mine. There is a pause. For a minute, I am her daughter again.

Then the moment passes and I slide back into my other role. I ask my mother what finally enabled her to accept "the elephant in the room"—the fact that I am sure her father abused me and she is sure he did not.

"I don't know if I should tell you this," she says. "I'm not sure you'll be able to handle it."

"It's okay, Mom," I say, "go ahead. I don't think you're going to say anything I haven't heard before."

Haltingly, she goes on. This time she is talking directly to me. The third person stuff has gone out the window. "I tried to believe the accusations, but I never could. I have searched my memory, and I've come to the conclusion that my father could never have done that to you.

"Then I read a lot of literature from the False Memory Syndrome Foundation. They described a profile of the typical survivor with false memories and you fit it one thousand percent. That was a big turning point for me. Instead of seeing you as my tormentor, I saw you as a person who was under the influence of people who had convinced you these memories were true. That helped me stop feeling that I had to protect myself and my family against you."

I am flabbergasted! This was not what I expected her to say. But at the same time, I am delighted by my mother's resourcefulness in finding a way to live with the unspeakable. Though I don't agree with her analysis, I feel no need to correct her. Instead, I say, "That's amazing—the False Memory Syndrome Foundation helped you make peace with me!"

"It did," she continues. "And then there was another incident that helped me see where my loyalties lay. I went to a False Memory Syndrome Foundation meeting. Someone got up and started attacking you and *The Courage to Heal*, and I immediately wanted to get up and punch the guy. No one there knew I was your mother, but I wanted to shout, 'How dare you say that about my daughter!' In that moment, I realized I felt much more loyal to you than I was to them. I picked up my pocketbook and left."

This time, I start laughing—imagining my mother at a False Memory meeting, revealing her identity as my mother and defending me to people who consider me their worst enemy. I am tickled by the idea and touched by her loyalty. "That's great, Mom," I say. "You should have let him have it!"

It's quiet for a while. We are both enjoying the

moment, relishing the extra space she has just created with her honesty. Then my mother asks, "How about if I turn the tables on you a little? Tell me, how have you come to accept the fact that I don't believe you?"

Being in this role is not as comfortable for me, but I know she has earned it, so I make my own attempt at setting the record straight. "I did a lot of hard work, Mom. I was in therapy for years. Then I moved here. I fell in love and had children. I got happier, and incest was no longer at the forefront of my life. It receded in importance, and I no longer needed you to believe me." I hesitate, knowing the next part is harder to say. "What it really came down to was that I looked at your life and realized that you couldn't afford to believe me. You grew up with him. He was your father. You loved him and you needed to remember him as a good man. I guess I finally accepted that."

I don't say more, and she doesn't ask. We look at each other, more love in our eyes now than there has been in years. We chat a little longer, I ask a few more questions, but the heart of our talk is over.

In our idiosyncratic ways, my mother and I each found a way to accept the unacceptable in each other. We have agreed to disagree. There are things we don't talk about, but we don't need to anymore. Around the elephant in the room, we have stretched out our hands, and our fingers are lightly touching.

Nietzsche and the
Ghost in the Attic

MELISSA SANDERS-SELF

my mother and I lived on Dwight Street in Berkeley in an old brown shingled two-and-a-half story California bungalow in 1969. I was in fourth grade and my mother Liza was a philosophy major at the University of California. She had a boyfriend called Nate, who lived with us. One rare afternoon when Liza was home and Nate was not, she passed me in the hall and told me she thought Nate was losing his mind.

"It's all because he borrowed my Nietzsche." She tossed her long hair back and I saw the letters float in my mind N-I-E-T-Z-S-C-H-E. I found it easy to remember the unusual combination of letters. I loved words. I didn't like what she was saying. "If he starts acting weird, ignore him. It's *Beyond Good and Evil*," Liza said, "it's putting him over the edge."

We both went to our rooms and that's where I was when Nate came home. He had people with him. I heard them talking downstairs. He and Liza had people over almost every night. Some of them were regulars, many of them only came once, traveling through Berkeley on their way to somewhere from somewhere else. They partied at our house smoking pot, discussing politics, literature, and philosophy while tripping and dancing to loud music. My mother loved to dance and I loved to watch her. I usually went to bed before the party ended and many mornings I woke up to sleeping bodies on every soft surface in the house.

I opened my door and listened for Nate. What did she mean about him losing his mind? He sounded like he always did, he was using his and-I-quote voice: "That which an age considers evil is usually an unseasonable echo of what was formerly considered good—the atavism of an old idea.' And guess what friends, there's a ghost upstairs in the attic of this house." What was he talking about? He did sound a little more excited than usual. I listened to Liza and her friends argue with him.

"You're so literal, so symbolically oriented..."

I shut the door. A ghost upstairs in the attic? I was intrigued. I liked Nate. He was home a lot during the day and it was nice to have someone else in the house. Liza was gone a lot. I usually came home from school and ate potato chips and read novels alone. Sometimes Nate kept me company sitting on the toilet during my bath. He passed me towels and dried me off and cuddled me close. Sometimes we wrestled and he tickled me on the bed. He never did anything I didn't like. He didn't try to put his tongue in my mouth or his fingers inside me. He would have showed me his penis if I was interested, because my mother and all her friends were into this back-to-nature Berkeley thing and everyone walked around naked inside our house, but I wasn't interested. What Nate did that I liked more than anything was sometimes when there was no party, he read to me and told me stories. He was a poet, and though I didn't understand half of the words he used inside his poems, I loved listening. My favorite was one he made from my name:

L Lovable little girl

U Unlikely

C Catalyst for change

Y You will always be special to me.

◄ ►

The next morning Nate asked me if I wanted to go with him to the Archives at the Berkeley Historical Society. A-R-C-H-I-V-E-S. I loved the word. I said yes.

"I decided to research the history of this house," Nate said as we walked toward Shattuck.

"Because you saw a ghost?" I asked.

"Did you see her?" Nate stopped and looked at me, excited.

"No, I heard you telling everybody last night."

"Oh," he started walking again, "I didn't tell you first because I thought you might be scared," he explained.

"Should I be scared?" I was thrilled. "What kind of ghost is it?"

"It's the ghost of a woman..." Nate said, allowing his words to trail away quietly.

"A woman? For real? When did you see her? What did she look like? Can she walk through walls?" Now I was excited. "Was she wearing a pretty long dress?"

"She was wearing black and she wasn't happy." Nate squeezed my hand and I realized we had reached the Historical Society. I followed him and settled into my own special heaven of words while he worked with the librarian. I stood reading in front of the largest dictionary I had ever seen. It was half my size and full of words I wanted to learn. I was in the Q's—quetzal; a bird from South America—when Nate came back. He had discovered a newspaper obituary from December, 1883. We sat down at a table in the corner and he read it to me in a hushed voice.

BERKELEY 1883 — No services are planned for the domestic Esther Porter, a poor unfortunate of unknown ancestry and no prior whereabouts, who passed away Sunday, December 31. Miss Porter had been recently dismissed from service by Mr. Edward Bennett of 21 Dwight Street after she allegedly caused the death of his infant daughter, Sarah, on Christmas Day. Miss Porter was arrested but had been released from custody in the Berkeley Jail house Saturday morning after the actual cause of death of the infant was determined by Dr. Cunningham to be pneumonia. Miss Porter was found dead on Sunday, at the new grave of the Bennett infant. Burial will be in Memorial Park, on a plot purchased by the Berkeley First Methodist Church for similar such unfortunate persons.

"This is her," Nate was certain this nursemaid was our ghost.

"How do you know?"

"The address. It's the same house, 21 Dwight Street. Besides, it makes sense, think about it." He told me the story he saw in between the lines of the newspaper facts. "The nursemaid, Esther, she used to live upstairs in the attic. It was Christmas time, so it was cold and maybe the Bennetts were entertaining, yeah, it was the parties. Esther loved little Sarah! She loved to hold her and dance around with her and she loved to hear her gurgling baby laugh." Nate was using his storytelling voice and I shut my eyes so I could see everything as he described it. "Esther hated to hear little Sarah cry, and when the Bennetts had their parties little Sarah cried until her face was red and everyone's ears were broken. Esther tried to calm the baby by taking her up to the attic, away from the party noise. But the cold came whistling through the wood lathe walls, it came through the cracks between the rafters and the shingles of the roof. The pneumonia started in the chilling cold, but the more ill she became the more the baby's cheeks burned like tiny red hot coals, until they burned out, turning white as ash. The doctors were unable to save her ... maybe they were called too late." Nate stopped speaking, looking like he wasn't quite sure which way to make the story go next.

"But why did she get arrested? Why was it her fault?"

"They had to blame someone, because ... because of

166

Mrs. Bennett. The wife. She was upset and angry. She couldn't stand the sight of Esther's flushed cheeks, or the sound of her coughing in the room above. She had no pity for her and the coughing reminded Mrs. Bennett of the child she had lost. She had no more child so she had no use for a nursemaid. She insisted Esther be charged, and taken away."

"But why would they do that?"

"It's the caste system, Lucy. Esther was just a paid slave."

"But the jail let her go."

"They had to, they didn't have any evidence against her. It was clearly an illness. I think Esther must have cried a lot in jail, in between coughing."

"Yuk."

"That's not the worst. The worst is the day she died. When they let her out of jail there was a cold fog lingering over Berkeley." Nate raised his hands above the library table top as if his fingers were the cold chilling fog. "Esther had no place to go, except to the fresh grave of the infant she had loved, where she succumbed to grief and her illness, and breathed her last." Nate sighed and I saw he was finished imagining the scene. "You know what, that was the same year Nietzsche published *Beyond Good and Evil*, I think I'm going to write a poem about this ... maybe I'll have Mrs. Bennett say 'God is dead.'"

"Why?" I asked, "Why would she say that?"

"Because she was angry, or sad, or an existentialist, or coming to terms with all the ways believing in God will be harder for her after the death of her baby. I don't know yet exactly why she might say that, I'm not sure what she'll say, but something..."

"Don't say 'God is dead.' It's not right, I thought God couldn't die..." I was confused but Nate started laughing.

"'God is dead' is something Nietzsche wrote, but he didn't mean it like you're thinking of it, he had a character who was crazy say it and he meant it in a much larger context." Nate was about to explain more but I didn't want to know about Nietzsche or his context. I was fascinated with the ghost.

"Do you think ... what you said ... do you think that's what happened? Really?"

"It says that's what happened, right here." He held up the photocopy of the newspaper as if he'd read his story off the page. "I'm taking this home for Liza. She doesn't believe I really saw the ghost."

"I believe you." I said. "I want to see her."

"No, you shouldn't want to see her. She's not happy."

"Well why did you see her?"

"I don't know ... maybe she's haunting me because she wants someone to tell her story. Or maybe it's because I'm a man, like Edward Bennett, who threw her out of the house."

"Next time you see her, ask her. Try to make friends

with her, find out what she wants." I thought this was a reasonable solution but Nate shook his head at me, like I didn't know what I was talking about. I didn't like that, but it didn't stop me from thinking my mother was definitely wrong, Nate was not losing his mind. Everything he said made sense to me.

◄ ►

Over the next few weeks I devoted myself to contacting the ghost. Everyday when I came home after school, I let myself into the empty quiet house, still and full of brilliant California sunshine, shimmering in light puddles on the dark wood floors. I ran straight up the first two flights of stairs and then paused at the wooden door to the attic and took a deep breath. I felt brave and powerful, capable of anything. I flung the door open and marched up the narrow twisting spiral stairs, pausing again at the top. Rays of sunlight held the dust trapped like Tinkerbell's crystal-pixie magic, floating in the air. I believed something magic could happen in that room.

"Ghost, please, Ghost of Esther Porter, appear to me," I said, at first in a whisper and then more loudly, walking solemnly through the rays of sun, my palms turned upward, trying my best to draw something special out of the unfinished walls.

I did this every afternoon for weeks but nothing materialized before me except some interesting thoughts. It occurred to me I wanted to be somebody special when I grew up. I wanted people to listen to me and to care about what I said. I didn't know what special thing I had to give to the world, but I thought I had something, and I thought maybe whatever it was, had to do with the ghost in the attic.

I went to the library and asked for books about ghosts. I found new words to love:

P-A-R-A-P-S-Y-C-H-O-L-O-G-Y

U-N-E-X-P-L-A-I-N-E-D P-H-E-N-O-M-E-N-O-N

I checked out a book called *Understanding ESP* and I read about Uri Gellor in Russia who could bend spoons using only the energy of his brain. I tried it, but I couldn't do it. The spoon remained unchanged, no matter how I willed it:

BEND.

BEND.

BEND.

I read about a yogi-magician in India who could levitate for twenty-four hours, and then I asked my friend Bucky to come over and help me practice. She was called Bucky for the obvious reason that her two front teeth were extra large. What I liked about her was the way she ignored the kids at school when they teased her. She laughed when they laughed at her, she tucked her black hair behind her ears as if she truly didn't care.

"Lie still." I took her up to the attic and made her lie on the floor with her eyes shut while I sat with her silky black hair resting in my hands under her head visualizing her rising off the ground. I watched the dust swirl in the sunshine and I concentrated. "Breathe lightly, think lightness, think, I am floating, above the ground."

"I am floating..." she repeated softly, following my instructions, breathing lightly. I noticed her relaxed lip was unable to close over her teeth.

"Floating..." I tried my hardest to raise her up.

It didn't work, but she swore she felt something. A tingling, along the edges of her body. I was encouraged enough to try something else.

"You sit here, and think really hard about an image. I'll sit across from you and see if I can draw what you're thinking."

"Okay, I'm thinking."

"Okay..." I closed my eyes and tried to reach into her mind and draw what I thought she was thinking. All I saw was black, but then I started drawing a tree and the head of a horse which happened to be what I knew how to draw best. Bucky opened her eyes and looked at my drawings.

"I was picturing my house and my dog in the yard," she said.

"That's not fair," I complained. "No wonder I didn't get it. You can't think of more than one thing."

"Why not? You were drawing two things, two things not even close to what I was thinking actually." Bucky was smiling, teasing me. "I like this game," she said.

"It's not a game. It's practice." I was frustrated with my lack of results.

"I'm developing my psychic powers so I can communicate with a ghost that haunts this house at night." I tried to be deliberately mysterious, stoic and brave all at once, implying she should be worried about what I was up to, worried enough to inquire, but Bucky wasn't even curious.

"Oh. That's cool. What do we do next?" She tucked her hair behind her ears expectantly. Sighing, I wished she would ask some questions, but I didn't want her to get fed up and go home early. I needed a partner to run the tests on me.

"Next we do a card test." I handed her a deck of regular playing cards Nate had given me and told her what to do. "Take a card and hold it up, so you can see it but I can't. I'll say if it's red or black, then you make one pile for when I'm right and one for when I'm wrong, got it?"

"Got it. Ready?" She held up the first card. Our first time through the deck it came out 28 to 24 in my favor, but I didn't think that was enough to prove I had psychic abilities worthy of developing. We did it again, and then again, and Bucky got more and more excited about it.

"I'm sending a thought message to you, the color of this card is..." said Bucky while shutting her eyes solemnly as if sending telepathic messages required closed eyes. I kept my eyes open, sometimes focused on the dust trapped inside the warm rays of sun. On my best try I guessed 41 out of 52. I liked focusing on the back of the card, letting the real image on the other side seep through into my brain. I felt again the warm expectancy, great things were waiting for me and my developing abilities when I grew up. Bucky thought so too.

"It's because I'm concentrating so hard, that's how come you're getting it." She believed it was her own ability to send the message, through her closed and concentrated eyelids.

"I can see through the card." I wanted to explain to her what knowing felt like. "It's like...I feel like, there's a pulse of energy that surges through me just for a second and then I can see the card."

"That's what I felt too, you got it." Bucky smiled and I smiled back, I had to, she looked so ridiculous when she showed all her teeth.

"Here, put your hands up." I held my hands palms out facing her and we sat feeling the energy surge between us. It was tricky feeling the heat radiating from our palms not touching. We ended up laughing too hard to continue.

◄►

I was still working at seeing the ghost and improving my psychic abilities when Nate began to say the nursemaid's presence was intolerable.

"'How many centuries does a mind require to be understood?'" He quoted from *Beyond Good and Evil* trying to explain what he saw.

"At night I hear her walking back and forth across the attic floor," he said.

It gave me shivers to think of a ghost pacing where I practiced developing my psychic powers. I was sorry I had not heard her, but I was a pretty solid sleeper.

Then, one night, I did wake up, hearing not the footsteps of the ghost in the attic, but Nate screaming.

"Stop it, stop it, I can't stand it anymore!"

"Stop what? I'm not doing anything! You're fine, there's nothing wrong."

Liza was shouting to be heard above his crying.

"Don't you hear her? Don't you see her?"

I jumped out of bed and ran to their room. I threw open the door and saw my mother holding Nate on the bed. She frowned at me.

"Go back to bed," she yelled because when Nate saw me he started yelling, "Do you see her? Do you hear her Lucy?" I had never seen him look like he did, his hair was standing up like pulses of energy were pushing out of his brain and his mouth was open, slack and frightening. I looked around the room, into the corners, up at the ceiling, expecting the ghost of Esther Porter but I saw nothing.

"Be quiet!" I yelled back, "I can't hear anything!" Nate stopped moaning and I tried to listen.

"Go back to bed," Liza snapped but I stood still listening. I heard my breathing and theirs, the house creaked, a siren sounded many blocks away. I heard the swish of the bedcovers sliding as Nate sank back, lying down. He spoke in his regular quoting voice:

"The greatest thoughts are the greatest events—are longest in being comprehended. The generations which are contemporary with them do not experience such events— they live past them. Something happens there as in the realm of stars. The light of the furthest stars is longest in reaching man, and before it has arrived, man denies—that there are stars there. How many centuries does a mind require to be understood?"

"Oh my God, fucking Nietzsche again. Will you please get out of here?" Liza was impatient and annoyed with me. I stood still trying to understand what Nate was saying.

"There is a regular cult of suffering!" he raised his voice.

"GO!" Liza hissed at me and I turned and ran, suddenly wanting nothing more than to crawl back in my warm safe bed and escape the cult of suffering. Whatever it was it didn't sound good. I could see the phrase floating behind my eyes, C-U-L-T O-F S-U-F-F-E-R-I-N-G. I wished I had seen the ghost or heard her footsteps. I wondered if reading Nietzsche would help?

◀ ▶

People still showed up at our house to party. A few nights after the night Nate woke me up screaming I heard people downstairs teasing him about the ghost.

"If she's really there how come you're the only one who

can see her?" This question came from Nate's friend, Jim.

"I have no idea. Did you bring the acid? Maybe we'll all see her tonight."

I stayed in my room and went to bed without going downstairs. They were listening to Jimi Hendrix and being noisy and I was really tired. While I slept, Nate's friend tripping in our attic thought he saw the ghost too. He said she was floating outside the attic window and he tried to jump out, screaming, "She says I can fly with her, I can fly! Let me fly!" Liza and everyone else there had to hold him down to prevent him from taking off. My room was under the window he wanted to fly from and I think I saw him in a dream, a shape with wings like Icarus, out of my school books, falling past.

I woke up sometime before morning when it was still dark. I don't know why I woke up. The whole house was quiet, everyone had gone home, including Jim who thought he could fly. Even Nate was asleep. I got up and walked to the bathroom at the end of the hall. I was sitting on the toilet when I saw the old brass doorknob turning, turning, but not opening. I jumped up and grabbed the knob and, opening the door, I saw the attic door halfway down the hall closing, and I felt a cold wind like the hem of a long dress, sweeping away. I thought I should run after her up into the attic to ask what she wanted and why she was here, but I was suddenly too scared. I ran to Liza's room and crawled into bed between her and Nate.

"Umm, why are you here?" Liza asked without opening her eyes when I pushed her over for more room.

"I think I saw the ghost," I whispered to her back.

"You didn't, there's no such thing." Liza's next breath was a snore and I lay staring at her back thinking I had never heard such an empty string of words.

◄ ►

The next day I got out my library books and read about the practice of making devotional altars. I spent all morning building one out of wood and bricks under my window. The book said to assemble candles, a chalice, power objects, herbs, and sacred texts for the altar. I went outside and cut fresh sprigs of rosemary, lavender, and sage from the garden. I took an old bronze vase Liza had bought at the flea market and put the herbs in it. I found an iron candlestick and a tall red candle, and I got out my crystal rock collection for power objects. I searched the book shelves by Liza and Nate's desks and returned to my room with a copy of Nietzsche's *Beyond Good and Evil* and a King James reference edition Bible. Liza stopped in my room to say goodbye before she left for class.

"What in the hell are you doing?" she asked, surprised.

"I'm making an altar..."

"With a Bible?" She was incredulous.

"I thought maybe I would start praying..." saying the words as I was thinking them. I hadn't made a plan to pray. I wasn't sure what I was planning to do.

"Jesus, Lucy that is so reactionary."

"What?" I didn't understand what she meant. R-E-A-C-T-I-O-N-A-R-Y?

"And Nietzsche? The last thing we need is another person reading Nietzsche. I told you, Nietzsche is what's making Nate act like a weirdo." She frowned at me then paused and sighed. I could see she needed to leave. "I'm late," she said, "I'll see you later."

She took off and I opened the Bible. I realized I was really scared. Seeing that door shut, feeling that cold wind, experiencing the ghost hadn't been how I'd expected it to be. It wasn't warm solid energy passing between my fingers and Bucky's, it was something cold and lonely. I remembered Nate at the Historical Society saying I shouldn't want to see her. Maybe he was right. I decided I would try to believe in God and see if it helped, and I read the Bible for the rest of the day.

◄ ►

I was still up in my room reading when the first people of the evening arrived. I went downstairs in time to hear Nate reading to everyone from *Beyond Good and Evil*, answering the question, What is a philosopher?

"A man who constantly experiences, sees, hears, suspects, hopes, and dreams extraordinary things; who is struck by his own thoughts as if they came from the outside, from above and below, as a species of events and lightening flashes peculiar to him; who is perhaps himself a storm pregnant with new lightnings; a portentous man, around whom there is always rumbling and mumbling and gaping and something uncanny going on."

"That's you, my friend." Nate's friend Jim was back to do it all again.

"How about we devote tonight to the free spirit?" Liza said, anxious to change the subject.

"How about some dancing?" suggested a woman I did not know.

"Yeah, no more heavy talk, let's groove." A man I had never seen before with a dark beard who looked surprisingly like Jesus pulled a joint from his shirt pocket and lit it. I walked through paisley and velvet legs, jeans and patchwork skirts parting like curtains for me. I looked for my mother and saw her putting a record on the turntable. I went to my favorite corner in the living room and sat down on the vinyl bean bag to watch for a while. They started dancing to The Jefferson Airplane and I listened to Grace Slick belt it out:

One pill makes you larger
And one pill makes you small
And the ones that mother gives you
Don't do anything at all

When Liza spotted me she came over and threw her long beads playfully around my neck like a rope. I liked dancing with her and I got up and everyone made space. I danced until I had to stop to get water and when I came back in the room they were all sitting in a circle cutting tiny little orange pills of LSD in half.

"I want to get really high," Liza said, "Give me a whole one."

I sat down again on the bean bag and someone changed the music. I watched my mother, Nate, and their friends dissolve into giggles, acting silly and laughing uproariously at each other. I started to laugh with them because they were funny; crazy grown-ups, laughing so hard over nothing.

The man I'd never seen before who looked like Jesus came and sat in front of me, kneeling against the bean bag. He stared very seriously into my eyes not speaking. I stared back, I liked this game, it was fun. I'd played it before. Who would break the stare first by blinking? Eventually it was me and I was surprised. I usually won.

"Tell me, what's the world like through the eyes of a child?" I heard his question echoing on the stereo. It was the chorus of a song by the Moody Blues.

"Pretty good," I answered immediately, thinking that was how it seemed to me in the moment. I smiled, realizing this was what I wanted; I wanted people to care about what I thought and realize I was somebody special whose thoughts mattered. All of a sudden I got this heavy and strange intuition about the future and what my life would look like when I was a grown-up, and I felt strongly it was not going to be pretty good later on.

"Pretty good," the man repeated soberly and I saw my simple response had disappointed him. He got up and left and I stayed where I was, watching the people stoned and stroking each other's necks, watching the smoke curl to the ceiling.

It was the middle of the night before I went to bed. I left when the people at the party started coming down. I watched them leave the living room and climb upstairs to the attic where they planned to gather in a circle on the dusty pillows to talk. I thought of the story Nate had told me about Esther Porter taking the baby into the attic to escape the party noise. I was sleepy and I turned in the hallway and went to my room. Because it was new I saw the altar right away under the window and I remembered Nate screaming about a cult of suffering. I stopped and put my hand on the Bible I'd left ceremoniously open. I thought of the man who looked like Jesus asking me how things looked through the eyes of a child. I prayed to God:

"If you exist and are real please don't let me forget I think things are pretty good."

I repeated this a couple of times, with mental effort for good measure, and when I finished I looked up and out my window, thinking maybe God was out there somewhere and maybe he was listening, and because of this I was in the perfect position to see Nate's body fly bottom first past my window.

I heard screams from the attic and the thud of him

landing in the bushes. For a minute I wasn't sure it was real but then I leaned forward, knocking the Bible and the candlestick off the top of my altar. I opened my window and looking out I saw him lying there all twisted on top of the lantana. I was vaguely aware of people shouting and crying and the roar of feet thudding behind me.

"Call 911!" I heard someone yell. I stayed at the window and watched until the ambulance came and took him away. He was unconscious but still alive. I heard the ambulance man say so. The man who looked like Jesus went with Nate into the ambulance. I watched Liza come back in to the house. She didn't speak to the police, but I saw other people did.

"It was crazy, he just, like, jumped, for no reason..."

Could that be true? Why would he jump for no reason? I met Liza in the hall on her way to bed.

"What happened? Is Nate okay? Are you going to the hospital?"

She didn't answer me. I couldn't tell if she was too upset or too stoned. She walked past me as if I wasn't there, reminding me of the ghost. I went back into my room and closed the door.

◄ ►

In the morning when I woke up she was at the kitchen table drinking coffee and packing her bag for school. She sighed when she saw me but I asked my questions as if we were already in the middle of a conversation.

"Why? Why did he jump? Did he think he could fly? Did he see the ghost?"

"There is no ghost!" she snapped and frowned.

"What happened? Tell me," I insisted.

"You're too young, you're not going to get it." She shook her head and her long hair fell forward hiding her face. I watched her struggling to fit her fat Existential Phenomenology book in the macramé purse. I loved the words on the spine, how long they were, how complicated. E-X-I-S-T-E-N-T-I-A-L P-H-E-N-O-M-E-N-O-L-O-G-Y. I saw the letters in my mind after they disappeared in her bag.

"How did it happen? Was it an accident?" I was not giving up until I knew.

"Jesus, just stop asking!" She sat down and took another sip of her coffee.

"What happened was Nate took too much LSD, basically. I think it was the drugs and the Nietzsche, that definitely had something to do with it, and lately he's had some bad memories surfacing," she paused. "Remember his mother?" She raised her eyebrows and looked at me.

We had visited Nate's mother in the summer. She lived in a cabin by a lake somewhere up north in the mountains. All I could remember about her was she looked a little like Phyllis Diller with white hair and an unhappy mouth. Liza kept talking.

"Since he's been taking LSD he's been going through

some stuff in his mind, some things he had forgotten that happened to him, like what happened last night was he remembered his mother with a martini in her hand, forcing him to lick her cunt when he was small. You know cunt, right? It's slang for vagina." Liza imparted this bit of information like she was telling me spuds was another name for potatoes. "Right before he went to the window Nate said he remembered his mother lying naked on his plaid bedspread when he was a kid—that same one she still has on that bed in his old room, where you slept." Liza smiled as if this was funny in some way I did not understand. I knew what a cunt was, but not a martini, and I couldn't understand why Nate's mother would ask him to lick her. Liza smiled devilishly, "Can you picture her saying, 'Come on baby, give me what you've got?' Fuck, no wonder he threw himself out the window."

"What?" I was confused. The image of Nate's body hurtling through the air came back to me.

"Pretty gross, huh?" Liza put her bag over her shoulder, ready to leave. "I was right, you aren't capable of understanding and I have to go."

"Is he going to be all right?" I asked thinking she was right, I wasn't capable of understanding. Who did understand all this?

"Who knows?" She shrugged, and I wondered why she seemed not to care. A normal person would care, I thought, angry with her and simultaneously wishing I did not care as much as I did.

"Was it because Nietzsche said God is dead?" I was serious, but Liza laughed.

"I doubt it, but maybe, in a larger context ... Maybe Nate looked around and the things he used to think were true he didn't believe in anymore, and maybe that's why he jumped out the window, but most likely it was the drugs. See you." She kissed me quickly on the cheek and took off without looking back.

Thursday Afternoon

NANCY ROBERTSON

knew something was wrong as soon as I saw Mom's drapes open and the house in darkness. Every evening at 9:00 Mom closed her drapes in the living room and front porch, and turned on the lamp on top of her television. It was already 9:15. The last day of August was almost over.

I didn't rush through the open gate and run up her wheelchair ramp. Thursday was her garbage collection day, and aside from leaving the gate open, the garbage men had left the lid separated from the can. I walked alongside the ramp, picked up the lid, set it firmly on top of the can, and placed the can back under the ramp. Every Thursday evening she asked me the same two questions:

"Did you put the garbage can back under the ramp?"

"Yes."

"Did you put the lid on?"

"Yes. Yes, I did."

I knew something was wrong and I knew not to run up the ramp and barge into the porch. The police cautioned me only a few weeks earlier. They had arrived before me when Mom activated the beeper on her emergency telephone, accidentally, again. She wore the beeper on a cord around her neck and at night tucked the beeper inside her pajama pocket over her heart. So it was at night when our telephone rang, severing dreams, releasing adrenaline, that I ran to answer the phone, hoping to interrupt the sequence of numbers programmed into Mom's phone before it woke her friend, Ethel, then her friend, Fran, and finally alert 911. Sometimes the ringing woke Bill and me four or five times a night. I heard the beep of the alarm as soon as I picked up the receiver. I squinted against the harsh overhead light in the kitchen as I punched the numbers on my phone to deactivate the alarm on Mom's phone and activate her speakerphone.

"MOM! MOM! ARE YOU ALRIGHT?" I hollered as loud as I could, trying to be heard over the alarm I knew was blaring in her living room. I don't know if she could hear the alarm or not. She always said, "I didn't hear a thing," when I arrived at her home in the middle of the night to push the button on her phone to stop the alarm. She would have had to sit up, transfer herself into her wheelchair, and work her way through narrow doorways into the living room to release the alarm herself. And she would have had to find light switches in the dark. It was probably easier staying in bed knowing I would arrive as soon as I dressed and ran the two blocks to her home.

"What are you doing here?" she asked when she saw me.

"Your alarm woke me. Are you alright?"

"Of course I'm alright."

By the second, third, or fourth episode, her response was, "I don't understand why the alarm keeps going off. There must be something the matter with that phone."

"I think you're accidentally pushing the button when you turn over, Mom," and I took the cord from around her neck and laid it beside her pillow. "Just leave it here while you are sleeping and put it back around your neck in the morning."

We went through the same conversation several times a night. Each time I arrived at her home the cord was back around her neck with the pendant tucked inside her pajama pocket.

One night, the constant ringing worked into my dreams. I couldn't get my legs to move, like a dream of being chased and not being able to run, dragging legs forward, willing every ounce of being to move quickly but not being able to move. A dream in which I could not get to the ringing phone. I don't know how long it took for me to wake, but I woke to silence. I jumped up and ran to the phone but I was too late—I got a dial tone. I phoned Mom but the line was busy. Then my phone rang.

"Nancy, does your mom live at 1019 Ninth Avenue East?" a friend asked.

"Yes."

"I've got my scanner on and the police were just dispatched to that address."

"I know. I've got to run. Thanks."

And I did know. I knew when I woke to silence. I knew when I heard the busy signal. I knew I couldn't keep up anymore. I knew I couldn't keep checking several times a day. I knew I couldn't keep running back and forth at night. And I knew she'd had enough. She apologized constantly for disturbing me, for being such a nuisance. "I don't know what's the matter with me," when she fell, when she burned her arm on the stove, when she knocked a lamp over, when she dropped a plate on the floor, spilt milk across the table, couldn't find her glasses, couldn't remember what day it was.

As quickly as I dressed and as fast as I ran, the police still beat me to Ninth Avenue. The flashing light on their car broke the stillness on the quiet street. I charged past the two officers walking up the wheelchair ramp and jammed Mom's house key into the lock.

"STOP! YOU DON'T KNOW WHAT YOU'RE GOING TO FIND ON THE OTHER SIDE OF THAT DOOR!"

I don't know if I stepped aside or if I was moved aside, but both officers entered the house ahead of me, gently and slowly opening the door into the porch, then the glass paneled door, covered with its crocheted curtain, into the living room. The alarm on the telephone blared louder as the doors opened. One of the officers stepped across the living room rug and pushed the flashing light on the telephone. When the alarm stopped, we could hear music pouring from Mom's bedroom filling every crack in her rundown wartime home. Scraped doorways, bashed furniture, marked walls were soothed by a piano and orchestra celebrating Beethoven's "Fifth Concerto."

Mom sat on the edge of her bed. The volume on her clock radio was turned up so loud she did not hear anything but the music. Her eyes were closed and her left hand kept the tempo exact with an imaginary baton. Her body swayed with the intensity of the music while her baton conducted the orchestra from pianissimo to forte.

The clutter in her room, photos, family mementos, knick-knacks, all came together like music made by different instruments in the orchestra. The two officers and myself stood in the bedroom doorway for several minutes while Mom conducted the musicians. The pianists fingers flew up and down the keyboard complimented by the crescendo of the orchestra. We stood quietly until Mom brought the "Emperor" to its conclusive ending.

There was a moment's silence. The red numbers on her clock radio read 11:59. I knew she would listen to the CBC news at the top of the hour before switching the button on the radio to start again at 8:00 AM. She liked to be up and dressed and have the drapes opened by 9:00 every morning.

One of the officers stepped into that silence. "Are you alright, ma'am?"

"What are you doing here?" she asked, and turning toward him she saw the other officer. Then she saw me. "Oh for goodness sake," she said. "Now what's the matter?

You're here too."

"Your alarm was set off again, Mom."

"How could that happen? What's the matter with that cockeyed thing anyway?"

"It's OK, ma'am. So long as you're alright, that's the main thing," said one of the officers as she patted Mom's arm.

"No, it's not OK. This is ridiculous. You shouldn't have to come and check on me."

"It's no trouble, ma'am. We're just happy that you're fine. But maybe you shouldn't be wearing your pendant at night. Why don't you put it beside your radio on the bedside table?"

"What good will that do me if I have to get up during the night and use the bathroom?"

"Do you use your wheelchair to get to the bathroom?"

"Of course I do."

"Why don't we tie the cord onto the handle of your wheelchair?"

Mom looked at me. She often deferred to me when questioned by others. It sort of crept up on me, this insecurity of hers. She wanted me with her for doctor's appointments, when the public health nurse visited, for assessments by health care workers, even when family arrived.

"I think that's an excellent idea, Mom. You always have your wheelchair next to you when you're not in it.

And you would be able to reach your alarm even if you fell transferring yourself."

"Well, OK, if you think it will be alright then." She lifted the cord from around her neck and handed it to the officer.

◄ ►

Finally a solid sleep. When my own clock radio woke me at 7:15, I couldn't figure out where I was. Within seconds I realized there was light around the edges of the blind. I sat up. Mom … I wondered if she was all right. I hadn't seen or talked to her for seven hours.

On my way to work at quarter to nine, I drove by her house. The drapes were still closed. I double-parked and ran up the ramp. I unlocked the door and let myself in. When I entered her living room, she was wheeling herself toward me.

"You again," she said. "What are you doing here? Aren't you supposed to be at work?"

"I'm on my way. Just thought I'd make sure you're OK."

"Of course I'm all right. Listen, you stop worrying about me. I'm fine. Now get going so you're not late for work."

"I'm on my way. Good-bye." I bent over and gave her a kiss. "I'll open the drapes in the porch for you on my way out."

"No you won't. You leave them alone. I'm perfectly

capable of doing that myself. I was just on my way to do that when you showed up. Now get going and leave me be."

"OK, Mom. See you later."

"Bye, Dearie. Don't you worry about me now."

For a few weeks a peaceful routine steadied our lives. Bill, who was working night shift, slept uninterrupted during the day, and I could hardly wait to go to bed at night to sleep the deep, dreamless sleep of exhaustion. I drove directly to Mom's after work, just like always, to take her for her walk up and down the wheelchair ramp three times. Then I practiced on the piano for a half an hour before going home and making supper. Bill and I lingered at the table before I packed his lunch and waved good-bye from our back porch window. After the kitchen was cleaned up, I walked downtown for a few groceries. I returned along the waterfront to look at fishing boats and net menders, and watch seine nets being overhauled. The late sunset over the harbor brought the days to a close and I walked back up the hill to a calm home and to a bed that beckoned with sweet, sweet sleep.

Mom still came for supper every Sunday and for special occasions. I noticed her struggle to get in and out of the car. She couldn't climb the three steps up to the front door without Bill helping her. All her clothes, everyday and Sunday best, displayed permanent food stains. She licked serving spoons. How could she get sloppy, this woman who drilled proper eating habits and table manners into her five children? "Sit up straight and eat properly!"

Sometimes there was a smell of urine in her home, so I would lecture her about getting up and going to the bathroom more frequently.

"But I don't need to go," she'd argue.

"Obviously you do Mom. I wouldn't say anything, but I know you don't want your friends smelling urine when they visit."

"Of course not! I'll be more careful."

I tried spending more time with her in the evenings so she could bathe more often. Either she didn't feel like it, or she was watching a special program on TV. "Oh, not tonight, Dearie." It was getting harder for me to make her care. And I knew she wasn't really safe anymore. But I had no solutions except to keep checking on her. I shoved the safety issue to the back of my mind and just ignored it. And I buried my head in sleep.

◄ ►

The last afternoon of August, Bill phoned me at work. He'd been asked to come to work at 6:30. "I'll get something to eat downtown," he said, "so you'll have time with your mother."

"No, then I won't see you. I can go over to Mom's after supper. I'll come home after work and we can eat together."

After Bill went to work I did the dishes. Then I sat down and read the *Daily News*. Quiet time alone in the early evening was a rarity and I felt lazy and relaxed and totally without any feelings of obligation or responsibility. I sat for a long time with my head back in the easy chair and my feet up on the footstool and let the pleasure of silence and stillness flow through me. I longed for solitude and beauty. I went for a walk into the lovely late summer evening, drawn toward the harbor and the sinking sun that was turning earth to gold and sky to crimson.

It wasn't until dusk settled in that I changed direction and hurried back up the hill. It would be too late to take Mom for her walk but time enough for a visit and a piano lesson.

My peace was shattered when I walked up Ninth Avenue and saw her house in darkness and the drapes still open. I knew something was wrong, but I didn't rush up the wheelchair ramp. I walked alongside the ramp, gathered the garbage can and the lid, and set the lid on top of the can. Once I had the garbage can firmly stowed away, I walked up the ramp. I carefully opened the door into the porch. It opened slightly, then came against some resistance. I put my head into the opening and saw Mom sprawled out on the porch floor. "Oh, Mom! Oh, Mom!" I repeated as I squeezed through the opening and into the porch.

"Nancy? Nancy? Is that you?"

"Oh, Mom..."

"Help me up, Dearie. Come here and help me up."

Her pants were wet with urine and there were two

small pools of vomit on the floor by her head. Her white hair was caked with dried vomit. Stepping over her, I ran to the bedroom, grabbed her pillow, and pulled a blanket from her unmade bed.

"I don't need that," she complained as I covered her body and slipped the pillow under her head. "Leave the pillow. You're going to get it all messy. I'm all right. Just help me up." She reached for the bar that Bill had installed beside the half step he had built for her.

"I can't Mom. You're too heavy for me. And you might have hurt yourself when you fell."

She was still saying she was all right as I was phoning 911.

While we waited for the ambulance, I sat on the floor beside her. Details of the accident filled me with guilt. She had not fallen at 9:00 in the evening; she had fallen at 9:00 in the morning after she had opened the drapes. She had lain on the floor all day knowing that I would come after work, the one day I didn't come on schedule. The one day I didn't check on her.

"Why didn't you reach up and push your alarm?" The wheelchair was right there in the doorway. I'd had to push it aside to get into the living room.

"I never thought of that."

"What about the mailman or the paperboy? What about the garbage men? They were here this afternoon."

"I must have dozed off for a few hours. I didn't hear

the mailman in the morning. I called out when I heard the garbage men but they were making so much noise they didn't hear me."

"But the paperboy. He threw the paper into the porch. He must have seen you."

"I know, Dearie. He asked me what he could do but I told him you would be here soon so not to worry."

I rode in the back of the ambulance with her. She hadn't wanted to go. Said she'd be all right if the ambulance attendants would just get her into her wheelchair. But with teasing and good humor, the medics convinced her that she must be hungry and sore after her twelve-hour shift. They knew just the place for her to get something to eat. Mom loved food. They must have known that when they had to get her onto the stretcher.

She was lucid and cheerful in the ambulance. She described her day. "It wasn't so bad. I dozed off and on all day. It really didn't feel all that long." She didn't complain about the long wait in the emergency room. "Why don't you go home, Dearie?" I'll be all right here." She answered all questions and told her story again. And again when she was settled into a ward. She was polite and appreciative to everyone. "Thank you. Thank you very much. You've been very good to me."

When all the paperwork was completed I looked at Mom lying back in the hospital bed. She seemed so old and frail, despite her two hundred pounds. Without her cluttered belongings surrounding her she looked so alone. White sheets, white walls, pale hospital gown. "Don't worry about her," the nurse said. "We'll take good care of her."

"I know you will," I replied.

When the nurse left, Mom took my hand. "Thank you, Nancy. You're so good to me. But I don't understand why I have to stay here. I'm perfectly capable of looking after myself."

"We'll know tomorrow if you have any broken bones, Mom. And you're too weak to be on your own. You've been twenty-four hours without anything to eat."

"I am rather hungry."

"I'll run along now. It's getting late and I have to work in the morning. But I'll see you tomorrow afternoon. I won't worry about you tonight. I know you're safe. Goodnight, Mom."

"Goodnight, Dearie."

I leaned over and gave her a kiss then put my cheek against hers. We stayed like that for several seconds. The pressure from her hand hurt my fingers as she tightened her clutch on my hand.

When I talked to her doctor the next day, he told me she was badly bruised on her right side but she had no broken bones. She was already asking him if she could go home. "I'll try and keep her here for a few days, Nancy, but I can't stop her if she wants to go."

I wanted someone else to make the decision that Mom

should no longer be in her own home. I didn't want it to be me. I didn't want to go back on my promise to her. But I didn't want to have sole responsibility for her anymore.

Knowing she was cared for day and night in the hospital brought relief to every waking moment. But at night dreams disturbed my sleep. No matter where I hid, Mom found me. Sometimes I was an adult hiding behind barnacle-covered pilings at low tide and sometimes I was a child crouched in a coal bin. One time Mom would be wearing her royal blue gown she wore when she played the organ at the United Church. Another time she would be in a coat she sewed together out of Dad's old suits. When she found me she started to fall over. I woke when I reached out to stop her fall.

In my *mind* I knew that Mom needed more care than I was able, or wanted to give. But in my *heart* I knew I could not make the decision to move her into a nursing home.

There was no reason for her to be in the hospital, and she wanted to go home, so she was discharged a week later. I picked her up and drove her home. I eased the car close to the curb and stopped right outside her house. I got her four-pronged cane out of the backseat and helped her out of the car and into her yard. She waited at the bottom of the ramp, clutching her cane and the railing and watched while I collected the lid and the can and placed the garbage can under the ramp.

"Did you put the lid on tightly?"

"Yes Mom, I did."

She clung to the railing and struggled up the ramp. She dragged her right foot onto the porch. "Oh, it feels so good to be home," she said as I helped her get her raincoat off and hung it on the coat rack. She grabbed the pipe railing and pulled her body up the half step and into the entrance of the living room. She turned her body, and hanging onto the railing with one hand, and the arm of the wheelchair with the other, she plopped into her wheelchair.

"Whew," she sighed with eyes closed. "That sure feels good."

I kept my mouth shut. I should have lectured her about the danger of plopping into her wheelchair. She had been taught after her stroke, and reminded regularly, to lower herself into the wheelchair.

"Have you got time to come in for a while?" she asked as she backed into the room.

"Sure. Have you had lunch? I put some leftovers in your fridge. Do you want me to warm them up for you?"

"No, I've eaten. Come and sit down. I want to talk to you about something."

I sat on the couch and she wheeled right in front of me till we were knee to knee. Her eyes lowered as she picked at a fresh stain on the front of her pale blue sweater. When she lifted her eyes she took my right hand in both of hers. She stroked the back of my hand while she talked.

"I want you to make arrangements for me to move

into The Manor. I want to stay here until the family visits this fall, but when the boys leave, I don't want to be alone. I can't keep it up anymore. It's too much for me. And it's too much for you. Will you help me."

Will you help me was a statement, not a question. And I couldn't answer anyway. I don't know if the emotion erupting inside me was relief or sorrow. Years of worry and frustration, and a lifetime of routines and memories tied together in her home, ended with the courage of her words. Her strength was my weakness. I could not keep myself together. Tears pooled in my eyes and spilled down my cheeks.

"Don't you worry about a thing, Dearie," she said, as she patted the back of my hand. "Everything will work out fine. Just you wait and see."

The Shoal Near Broken Cliffs

PETER REESE

erek woke well before dawn, his heart running quickly. The apartment was dark and silent but for the radiator's intermittent rattle. He went to the bathroom and filled the tub. Lowering himself into the steaming water, he groaned at the heat. It took a long time to submerge his head. The sound of sloshing filled his ears and the hairs on his arms and chest swayed in the faint current.

As a small boy, Derek had believed he could breathe underwater. He learned by age four to work the faucets and only stern parental efforts could get him out of the bath. Beneath the heaped soapsuds, he imagined a kingdom of clouds. The water moving in and out of his mouth felt like air.

Now, a pressure rose in Derek's chest, as if the oxygen was expanding and would burst his lungs. But he could stay under a long time. The trick was to stay detached and keep your eyes closed. He tried to breathe the water. Finally, it was too much. He came up, gasping.

He stayed in the tub about an hour, thinking about his wife. She and their son Tommy had been gone for three days. When the windows lightened, he got out. He was dressing when his cousin's truck stopped outside. Derek picked up the long fishing rod. His belly cramped, something he should take care of before getting to the boat, but there wasn't time. As he descended the stairs, the rod protruded and bounced like a jousting pole and scratched the slanted ceiling. Sarah would probably notice that, but he wasn't sure when she was coming home.

A series of honks disrupted the morning air. Derek shook his head and put the tackle into the flatbed. Jay was chomping at the bit as usual. In the cab, Derek detected the odor of fish and mildewed clothes. His cousin pointed to a coffee cup lodged in the flimsy drinkholder.

"Top 'a tha marnin' to ya," he said in an unconvincing brogue. "That's yours."

"Thanks. How did it look out there?"

"Kind of blowy when I crossed the bridge, but it's supposed to calm later," Jay said. "Good to see you, cuz. Let's catch us some fish." He pulled onto the boulevard. Broken pink cirrus clouds moved fast between rooftops.

"Smells like a bait shop in here," Derek said.

"Goddamn perfume!" Jay said, slapping the steering wheel. "I call it 'Striped Bass Deluxe.' Fifty bucks an ounce. But I can maybe cut you a deal." He grinned. Well over six feet and big boned, Jay seemed to barely fit in the truck. He had thick hands and chipped, gray-tipped nails. At thirty-five, his brown hair had thinned into a peninsula that tapered near his forehead. His long face framed a nose sizeable enough to cast a shadow in bright light, earning him the nickname "Sundial." But Jay had never suffered a shortage of girlfriends.

"You look tired," Jay said.

"I didn't sleep much. Probably too quiet in the house. Usually we're up with the baby once or twice," Derek said.

"Well, drink your coffee. No snoozing in the boat." Jay chuckled. The impossibility of sleep was a given in the jostling outboard on a brisk September morning. "Sarah's down at the Cape? Worked out nice that you got the morning free."

"Our place needed a bit of painting. So she took Tommy there to escape the fumes," Derek said. He slurped some coffee, his nostrils filling with a cloying vanilla. His belly made a high-pitched noise and a cramp followed. The truck shook as it climbed the on-ramp to the elevated highway. They made good time to Gloucester, catching green lights in succession through the miles of used car lots. When they passed the boarded-up bait shop, the conversation turned, as it usually did, toward Derek's father. Derek's father had owned a boat, "Ebb Tide," and used to take them out frequently when they were boys. They still fished many of his father's favorite rips and shoals.

"You remember when I stole a beer from your dad's cooler?" Jay said.

"The same day you let go of the rod."

"Yeah. I was three sheets to the wind after about two sips."

"Well, what's new?" Derek said.

Jay shook his head. "I was twelve. I think it was Pabst Blue Ribbon. Still hate the stuff. The diesel and the heat finished me off."

"You puked all over. I think it's what got the fish biting."

"I should try that more often," Jay said. "Hey, what was her name? Your dad's red-haired girlfriend. She was good to me that day."

"Carol," Derek said. "She was alright."

Carol was the girlfriend Derek's father had kept the longest, probably six months. She had worked hard to befriend the boys, packing them peanut butter and marsh-mallow sandwiches. Derek remembered her worn cotton T-shirts; his father used to tickle her by poking his finger into the mothholes. Carol could put away plenty of Pabst, and she wasn't afraid to stand up to Derek's father either.

"Hell of a pair of lungs," Jay said, cupping his hands to indicate breasts.

The day Jay dropped the rod, Carol had covered for him. The rod and its expensive reel had disappeared instantly into the bright blue water. Derek's father, a short and broad-chested man with biceps as hard and thick as a lamppost, had emerged irate from the cabin. Curly, auburn hair coated nearly every inch of his body save his fore-head. Jay turned pale as styrofoam. Derek stared at the receding waves and contemplated jumping in. But, Carol claimed she had bumped into Jay and knocked the rod from his hands. "Blame it on me, Captain," she said, spreading her red manicured nails across his sternum. "It was an accident."

"He had a temper," Jay said. "But shit, the man had skills." Derek's father had had an unerring sense of where the stripers would run. He had three boxes of lures, and the inscrutability of his choices (target fish, season, weather, wind direction, rumor, the smell of the wind) bordered on the astrological. In the boat, his father was always restless, one hand on the wheel, the other on his beer, scanning the horizon and the chart, following the fishermen chatter on the radio. They always caught something.

◄ ►

Derek and Jay got to the marina and carried the rods and coolers onto the pier. Gulls shrieked and wheeled around two lobsterboats that worked the mouth of the harbor. Hundreds of sailboats and pleasure cruisers rocked on the moorings, and the regular clink of a loose halyard blown against a mast kept rhythm with Derek's feet. They rowed a dinghy out to Jay's seventeen-foot outboard, "Butter Side Up." The outboard was sturdy and cream-colored, with rusted guardrails and numerous scuffs marking encounters with "bricks," as submerged stones were called. The sun warmed Derek's shoulders as he clambered from the dinghy into the bigger boat.

Jay and Derek had done a lot of fishing in "Butter Side Up," and also visited the islands in Boston Harbor. Sarah had come on a few of those island trips, although she had a tendency to get seasick. She and Jay got along well; he appreciated her caustic sense of humor. She ribbed him about his boat's name, which referred to a piece of toast that lands the right way after a fall from the breakfast table. Sarah called the boat, "Lunch Comin' Up."

The last time she'd come, there was chop, and Sarah had wanted to turn around. She and Derek had argued. "I'm nauseated. It's the worst feeling," she had said. "Why can't you understand that?" But it was Jay's birthday and there were five others with them. It was an inconvenience to everyone to go back. She was stubborn. Derek left her alone in the bow of the boat, her knees pulled up to her chest. In the end, Jay had noticed Sarah wiping away tears, asked Derek about it, and insisted on turning around after all. The next week, Sarah figured out she was pregnant. It had taken Derek by surprise.

◄ ►

Derek pulled the waterlogged rope off the cleat and the boat was free. Jay steered a circuitous route through the multitude of moorings. They motored slowly out of the marina, the waves clucking at the hull.

"Hey, tell me what it's like being a father," Jay said.

"Tommy's great. He's learning how to laugh."

"Six months old! Last time I saw the kid you could fit him in a lunch box," Jay said. "I can't wait to have a son of my own."

"My advice is you start with a girlfriend. Then work your way up."

"Details, details," Jay said. "I know taking care of a baby is hard work. You probably get stressed every time he gets a cold. But you two seem to be handling it."

Derek swigged water from the bottle.

"How's Sarah?" Jay asked.

"Alright," Derek said. "It can be hard sometimes. Not sleeping gets to her. The thing is that Sarah can't stand hearing him cry. We're up most nights."

"Must have brought you two a lot closer."

"I don't know." Derek took another gulp and washed down a lump of bagel. "You see a different side of each other."

◄ ►

Jay leaned on the throttle as they rounded the jetty. The boat slammed against the water, which felt hard as concrete, then began to hydroplane. The air tugged at their shirts and their hats and the skin of their faces. Derek's stomach twinged and then settled. The morning had autumn's startling clarity, the visibility nearly endless as if summer's residue had been scoured away. Jay was aiming for a shoal off a steep stretch of coast Derek's father had called Broken Cliffs.

Derek remembered his first trip to the shoal after his parents split up. He had refused to see his father for six months. Finally, his mother had forced the issue. She had driven to the marina on a Sunday, reached across him to open the passenger door, and pushed Derek into the parking lot. Derek had inhaled dust agitated by the tires, and made a show of coughing. He glared at her through the car window. "Fine," he said.

"Fine is right," she replied, not without tenderness. "The man's an asshole, but he's your father." She left.

Derek sat on the gravel for a while, but thirst propelled him toward the creaking and somewhat dilapidated dock. The marina was all men, washing the hulls with sudsy tan sponges, staining the floorboards with bitter scented oils, drinking beer on frayed lawn chairs. He saw his father, who was restringing one of the fishing rods, on board his boat. "Ebb Tide" was a meticulously maintained, twenty-five-foot motorboat, with a spacious stern and a small pilothouse paneled with glossed wood. Derek stopped about fifteen feet away. Intent, his father didn't seem to notice. The muscles in his father's forearms tensed like cables and Derek reflexively tensed his own, wondering if his eleven-year-old body would ever fill out. He was one of the smallest kids in his class and it bothered him.

"Hey Sam, is that your boy?" a man yelled from another boat.

"Yeah," his father said without looking.

Derek scowled at the other man, then moved slowly to the stern of "Ebb Tide."

"You want to fish?" his father said.

"I don't know."

His father cleared his throat, put down the rod, and finally regarded his son. His father had a chin dimple and cheeks so round it looked like he might spit water, adolescent features which offset the profound hairiness of him. The man's five o'clock shadow felt coarse enough to sand down a brick, and today he had several days' stubble. "You grew," he said.

"Not really."

"The stripers are running."

"I don't care."

"Then stay here," his father said. He opened a floor hatch and leaned his torso into the sunken engine chamber. "Hey, hand me the crescent wrench," he said, his voice resonating.

Derek contemplated the request, then climbed aboard, got the wrench from the toolbox, handed it to his father, and returned to the pier. The moan of a reluctant bolt merged with cursing, and then his father emerged from the hole. Derek folded his arms, putting his fists beneath his biceps to inflate their size.

"I want to say something."

"Go ahead." His father sat on the gunwale and rested the wrench on his lap.

210

"You try to hit Mom again, you have to go through me," Derek said. His feet were sweaty and slippery within his shoes, and he felt off balance. He rested his palm on a wooden guardrail and promptly got a splinter.

His father nodded several times. "Go through you. All right. I see you mean that."

"Shit yeah."

"Watch your mouth," he said. "Anyway, you won't have to worry about it. Your mom and I, that's part of the past now."

"Fine," Derek said.

His father began pulling in the rotund, orange fenders that protected the boat from collision with the dock. He stood the rods in white plastic sleeves along the cabin, then paused with a smaller one. "You might have luck with this," he said.

After his father disappeared into the pilothouse, Derek picked at the splinter, which wouldn't budge. He looked around at the other men on the dock, wondering if he'd come across as a fool. Finally, he got back on the boat. The striped bass went wild that day. In the slack water near the shoal, the stripers looked like they were tearing bites out of each other's backs to get the lure. Their silvery bodies leapt and splashed, and even once caught, they thrashed in the netting. "Look at 'em shine!" his father shouted. He held the slick fish in the sunlight for a moment before depositing them in a small tank beneath the floorboards. Every now and then, the uneasy sounds of sloshing water and muscular tails beating against the compartment were audible beneath their feet.

◄ ►

At the shoal, the tide's ebb opposed the incoming waves. These watery forces mingled and contended, churning out foam and brief eddies, finally plunging toward the rocky bottom as if to settle their dispute out of sight. Jay eased off the engine while Derek heaved the anchor and its length of corroded chain. The current swung the boat sixty degrees before the anchor made fast. They put on their sunglasses and readied the rods.

"I hear the fishing wasn't half bad this summer," Derek said.

"Yeah. The stripers are really coming back. The limits are what saved them. Guys were taking too much."

"People would fish until the seas were empty," Derek said.

"I wish you could have made it out here more," Jay said.

"It's hard to get away."

They cast along the shoal's contour. Jay used a tall surf rod and sent the lure tumbling through the air sixty feet before it glanced off a wave and disappeared. The churning water had a way of putting phantom tension on the lures, and they had some false alarms.

They debated the choice of lures. Derek remembered his father telling the boys to "think like a fish." Instead, Derek had imagined himself as a boy in the ocean, sucking the frigid sea into his lungs, taking refuge from the current behind the dark bulk of a stone. He pictured the shiny lure wiggling past, trailing a red beaded tail like a kite's.

"You know, when I was a kid, I used to think I could breathe underwater," Derek said, reeling.

"Oh yeah?" Jay said.

"I was convinced. Used to hold my breath in the pool for a long time, probably minutes."

"Well, maybe your kid will grow gills. Take after his old man," Jay said.

Derek thought of Tommy the last time he had seen him, in the crook of Sarah's arm, wearing a small black knit cap, blinking at his mother's face. What would a six-month-old remember? He wasn't sure how much the boy could even see, if he could discern features or skin tone, a swollen lip or a bluish crescent. Derek's stomach pained him suddenly, a sharp and focused pain, as if a rodent was burrowing his way out.

"His old man," Derek repeated. He casted at the cliffs, which were steep and serrated, with two large breaks that framed wedges of sky. The cliffs had the uneven color of a bruise, streaks of russet, umber, and a purplish blue, discernible as they approached the water's edge.

Suddenly, a yank on Derek's line announced the hunger of a fish. Jay whooped. "Keep the tip high! Let her run a bit." He casted into the same stretch of water. Within moments, the surface broke as if pelted by a fierce and invisible rain. Jay's line crossed the school, but couldn't get a bite. He kept casting.

Derek worked the fish, trying to be patient. The fish made for the cliffs, but Derek coaxed him toward the boat. He hoped for a striped bass. The bluefish had sharper teeth and could break a line without a metal leader near the lure. He reeled steadily, trying to find a rhythm that would soothe the fish. When the fish got closer, Derek glimpsed a long dark curve in the green shadows, but then it dove again. The ocean magnified and distorted everything. The fish swam into the shoal and Derek adjusted his hands. He lowered the tip momentarily, and then suddenly the tension fell away.

"Gone?" Jay asked.

"Lost her," Derek said. He knew before getting to the line's end that the lure was gone as well.

"Oh, man," Jay said. "Must have been a bluefish." He kept casting while Derek fastened a leader onto his line. He imagined the fish settling toward the bottom, the lure hanging from his mouth. It would rust. They had caught fish with fragments of old lures in their cheeks before. Sarah had once watched Derek reel in such a fish, and it was one of the things that had turned her off to fishing. He had told her that fish couldn't feel things in their mouth; they didn't have nerves there. A fish could survive a long time like that. But it didn't make any difference to her. She wasn't coming back.

Derek finished tying the leader and sat on the gunwale.

He had lost the desire to keep going. Turning toward the sun, he shut his eyes. He didn't want to fish anymore, but he didn't want to go home.

Jay kept getting bites, but none would stay.

"I might have more time this fall," Derek said. "Maybe we could come back here."

"Yeah?" Jay said. He stopped reeling and looked at Derek, the churning water reflected in his sunglasses.

Derek said nothing.

"Alright," Jay said finally. "Hey, I always think about your dad when I see the cliffs."

Derek nodded, casting into the shoal. You could easily get snagged in there, but he wanted to feel the water's force on the line. "I don't want to talk about my father anymore," he said.

"Alright," Jay said, chewing on his lip. His rod was bending toward the waves, but he kept the tip high. Rocking slightly on his feet, Jay's face relaxed. He played the fish back and forth across the stern. Derek got the net and waited. There were hints of something in the depths.

The Nickname

SHARON BRAY

i walk through the doorway of the home and look for her. A dozen faces turn toward me. "Hello," someone calls tentatively. I smile and say hello to the elderly faces whose eyes meet mine. A few reply, but most of them seem unaware of me and stare at the floor.

Where is she? The nurses told me they would have her ready. My eyes search the small lobby, and I see her at last. She is dozing peacefully in a chair near the television, her hands folded across an open book. She no longer can read, but she remembers that it once distinguished her from her poor rural beginnings. Even now, she still has her pride.

The staff has taken pains to dress her for my visit. Her silver hair is neatly trimmed and brushed away from her face, framing it as a remembrance of the lion's mane she used to have. Her cheeks are colored with a light touch of rouge, and her lips are outlined with soft pink lipstick. She sits, head nodding onto her chest, with all the others, their faces wiped clean of expression. My heart aches. This is where my mother lives, locked inside the fading memories of her past and the small, manicured grounds of a home for Alzheimer's patients.

She hasn't noticed me yet even though I'm hard to

216

miss. Tall, and holding a massive bouquet of bright pink azaleas in my arms, I look strangely out of place. I walk over to her and smile, "Hi Mom." I bend to kiss her cheek as she opens her eyes and slowly turns toward me. Her blue eyes are cloudy. She searches my face; the effort to remember shows in her furrowed brow. For a moment, she seems not to know who I am. This hasn't happened before, and a lump forms in my throat. Then her face brightens with a flash of recognition.

"Well my goodness," she speaks slowly, struggling for words. "It's my sister Dolly."

A nurse corrects her. "No, Oweta, it's your daughter Sharon."

I laugh and tell my mother that I'm happy to be whoever she wants me to be, that Dolly is a fine name. I hold the azaleas out to her. "I brought you some flowers."

"Oh my goodness," she smiles and slowly shifts her gaze to the profusion of pink blooms. I hand the bouquet to the nurse, who tells me she will put them in a vase and take them to my mother's room. Mom stares at the flowers. I touch her wrinkled hand to get her attention. "Mom, let's go sit outside on the patio." I offer my hand to help her stand, but she seems intent to do it alone. Her knuckles are white as she grasps the arms of the chair. She labors to raise her body into a standing position. I do not remember her being this weak when I last visited her just two months before.

Mother holds my arm tightly, and we walk slowly toward the double glass doors that open onto the small patio. I am shocked by her deterioration. All of her life, my mother loved to walk, priding herself on her straight, erect posture, striding forward with vigor and determination. Now she seems uncertain, unsteady on her feet, and she moves forward in small, shuffling steps. The nurse tells me that she has begun to use a walker. I hide my dismay with cheerful banter as we make our way outside. I guide her to one of the white vinyl chairs and ease her gently into the seat. Sitting down across from her, I take her hands in mine, "How are you Mom?" I ask.

She slowly turns to look at me again, carefully appraising my face. "Dolly," she murmurs, "my sister Dolly." I do not correct her. I learned the futility of that long before now. Instead, I take her hand and hold it in my own. She smiles and closes her eyes, raising her face to the sun. I let the silence float between us. She has never before mistaken me for anyone else. This will not be the last time. But Dolly? I start to smile, remembering a long forgotten time when I would have given anything to be called something other than my given name of Sharon.

It was the late fifties, and I was in seventh grade. Junior high school was a time of nicknames. All my friends had them, those cute, shortened versions of their birth names: Jen, Becky, Judy, Bobbi, Buck, and Gordie. I was simply known as Sharon, and next to the trendy, shortened

218

versions of my friends' names, mine seemed stiff and formal. Boring. I longed for a nickname.

I began my search, trying out several names, covering entire notebook pages with carefully scripted possibilities and whispering each quietly as I lay in my bed at night. After many nights of deliberation, I chose one and decided to introduce my family to it at the dinner table the following evening.

Five of us were seated around the chrome table in the kitchen: Dad, Mom, my younger sister, Darilyn, my brother, Craig, and me. I waited until my father had given thanks for our meal, then I cleared my throat. I had something important to say.

"Ahem." My parents and my siblings looked up from their plates, their eyebrows raised quizzically. I made my announcement. "I've chosen a nickname for myself. From now on, I'd like everyone to call me by it." I smiled triumphantly.

"That's very nice dear," my mother replied. "And what nickname have you chosen?" All eyes were on me, the silence broken only by the sounds of my younger brother as he took a big swallow of milk from his glass.

"Dolly," I declared proudly. "I'd like to be called Dolly."

For a moment, no one said anything, but then disaster struck. My father lowered his head, his face twitching with suppressed laughter. Mother put her hand over her face and tried to look serious. My sister giggled and nudged my brother. He exploded with laughter, sending a mouthful of milk across the table and onto our plates, drowning my vegetables and rice. "Dolly!" he shrieked. "Dolly!" At that, everyone was laughing, that is, everyone but me. I was humiliated. I stood up and pushed my chair away from the table, stomping angrily out of the kitchen and down the hallway to my bedroom. I slammed the door. It had not gone as I expected. Red-faced and embarrassed, I sat alone on my bed, fingering the fringe of my chenille bedspread. How could I face them again? I heard a soft tapping on my door.

"Sharon, can I come in?" It was my mother.

"Y-y-y-yes," I snuffled loudly.

She opened the door, walked toward me, and gently put her hands on my shoulders. "Honey," she said softly. "We're sorry. Really. It's just that ... well, we were just a little surprised, that's all." I squirmed and pulled away from her. "We love you and your real name, but if you want to have a nickname, then you can have one." She patted my shoulder. I softened. "Please come back and join us for dinner."

I followed my mother back to the table and sat down. My father dished up new supplies of vegetables and rice onto my plate. I picked up my fork. "Dolly," my brother snickered under his breath, then he let out a yelp. "Ow!" He turned to glare at my sister who had just delivered a swift kick to his shins.

"Children..." my father warned. We finished our meal in silence. No one said anything about my nickname again, and later, as I lay awake in bed, I decided to give up on the whole idea. I was not going to risk any more embarrassment, especially from my classmates. So I reluctantly settled into my given name. Sharon. Sharon Ann, if my mother was irritated with me. No one in my family ever did call me Dolly. At least, not until now.

"My goodness," I hear my mother say again, "my sister Dolly." She smiles and nods. Her eyes are closed, and her face is still turned toward the warmth of the afternoon sun. She remembers a younger, happier time. I do not disturb her. I sit quietly and hold her hand.

Dolly. I smile. Not a bad choice, actually. I stroke her hair and softly kiss her cheek. "I love you, Mom. Dolly loves you."

Runaways

ASHLEY SHELBY

among assorted ticket stubs and notecards that I keep pinned to the bulletin board above my desk is a photograph of my mother. In the photograph, she is standing on the outdoor platform of the train station in Stratford-Upon-Avon in England. She has placed her large red hiker's backpack on the bench in front of her. Minutes before I snapped the picture, she had unzipped the bag and clawed through its contents frantically, searching for items of clothing that could be abandoned before we stepped on to the train to London. By the time I had actually pulled out the camera to document what I believed was, after two weeks in England, the breathtaking zenith of mother's madness, she had already stuffed a pair of ratty black stretch pants into a large gap in one of the pillars supporting the platform's roof.

I keep this photograph pinned to my bulletin board not so much as a memento of our trip to England, but as contrast to the picture I've placed next to it—a photograph of my mother as a modish, stunningly beautiful young woman with thick dark hair, large brown eyes, and a tender, diffident expression on her face. She is standing in front of a Christmas tree, holding a bottle of Old Granddad bourbon—

a twenty-first birthday gift—in front of her like a religious offering. I've paired these photographs because they represent a narrative that, at some point in time, had diverged. One, with its history of holiday snapshots, tight Capri pants, and slim menthol cigarettes, had ended abruptly at some unknown point in time. The other, a postmodern tale of concealed discontent, aggressive idiosyncrasies, and existential slovenliness, had flourished, and was the story of my mother that I knew by heart.

My mother and I were participants in an uneasy friendship, one established on the milder sides of adolescence, for me, and menopause for my mother. As a child, I was labeled by child psychologists as "difficult" and "emotionally labile"; they considered my mother "tentative," with "poor instincts." Later, when she was no longer engaged in compulsory mothering and I was bored with petulance and resentment, we found these succinct psychological biographies humorous. It seems we had been exquisitely mismatched or, if you were particularly fascinated by the physics of animosity, extraordinarily well matched. We were uncomfortable around each other. I thought, for many years, that my mother simply didn't like me. She wrapped my two younger sisters in affectionate embraces many times in a day. I received hugs only upon returning home after a long absence, and only because other family members were present and it seemed the right thing to do. When my mother and I were obligated to hug, we leaned into it precariously, leaving a large gap between our midsections. My friends who witnessed our rare hugs called my mother "the flaming pole" because that's how I embraced her. Living away from home, though, softened my impressions of my mother, and time and distance seemed to erase the notion my mother had of me. As we both grew older, we tried to dismiss our former hostilities as rumors.

The olive branch had come in the form of an invitation from my mother to accompany her to Disneyworld one spring. I was a freshman in college and should have been following the herd to some Mexican resort town or to a Florida coastal city, but my first years of college were not much different from my years in high school. I never seemed in the loop. Everyone had been surprised that we took the trip together, and somehow we'd managed to have a good time. It was the first trip we'd taken alone together. My mother bought me trinkets—a charm bracelet, a stuffed animal, a sweatshirt. She got drunk at a Spanish restaurant in the Epcot Village and as we exited the park around closing time, she clung to my arm and I felt a little uncomfortable. The trip, however, was a success because we did not fight. Since then, travel has been the conduit through which my mother and I conduct the business of being mother and daughter.

In that spirit, we'd decided to take a trip to England. My mother had liked the idea but said she had to talk to

"Frick and Frack" to get things settled at the travel agency and then had to get the "snips and snaps" of the accommodations in England set. But most importantly, she needed to start planning out the packing design. My mother is a militant packer—she takes pre-vacation sorting very seriously. Before our trip to England was even ticketed, she had drawn a strategic map marked with possible land mines (should the toothpaste go into the side zipper with the earrings, or would that leave us with a pierced tube?) and delegation of troops (the front will push forward with the sweaters while the second battalion will linger behind with the underwear—if we lose a few, we'll survive. We can turn the remaining undies inside out). She made it clear that she was "packin' light."

Since we planned to bike, my mother insisted that we bring along a pair of futuristic bike shorts, with a crotch protector built in. Held in hand, the shorts cut a frightening figure. The back end was stiff with its nylon and cardboard diaper and the fabric was slick and dangerously adept at harboring static electricity. Not necessarily a feature one looks for in a pair of skin-tight surrogate underwear. My mother would also find room for her portable apothecary, stowed in an oversized Ziploc bag—hormone pills, anxiety pills, and heart medicine. The contents of that Ziploc bag were now strewn across the bureau in room three of Badminton Villa in Bath, England.

The fog had been hanging thick and low over the

short-stacked city of Bath when we arrived. My mother
and I had been headed to a bed and breakfast somewhere
on the southern slopes of the valley and were waiting for
our host to pick us up. A tiny red Volkswagen puttered its
way through the heavy mist and honked at us cheerfully.
John, a paunchy bald man, was uncomfortably pinned
between the steering wheel and his seat, but he was smiling and waving us in.

"Hello girls," he shouted. "Put your bags in the back
and hop in." When we arrived at the inn, John sat us
down in the drawing room. "Bath is a tea saucer, if you
think about it," he said. He owned Badminton Villa, along
with his wife Sue. They were a middle-aged couple, whom
we rarely saw together. "And anyway, a tea saucer curves
upward doesn't it? Well if you think about it, our little
place is situated on this side of the tea saucer." My mother
and I had leaned toward him and studied the invisible tea
saucer he was holding delicately in the palm of his hand.
"And you really must take the Mad Max comedian's tour
of the city," he said. "Hilarious. Tears rolling, roaring with
laughter. Absolutely roaring." I roared with fake laughter
because John was laughing and I felt obliged to find the
English as funny as they sometimes found themselves. But
my mother had no tact—how dare she not fake laugh? Not
even a fake smile for his troubles.

When we finally escaped from the living room, my
mother spent ten minutes in the bathroom, brushing her

teeth, hacking up phlegm and washing her underwear in the sink. When she emerged, she was rosy-cheeked and composed in the way people are when they are in the full swing of their nightly ritual—maybe even a little giddy because she'd discovered this ritual could be completed on foreign soil. The ritual continued. Before getting into her bed, my mother had to check the windows and her underwear drying on the sill, take her hormone pills lest another whisker appear on her chin, check under her pillow for her book (*Auntie Mame* by Patrick Dennis) and, as a kind of final flourish, scratch herself like a baseball player about to take the plate. She performed this last particularly unsavory act to force an exasperated, disgusted sigh from me, which was usually produced promptly. My mother liked nothing better than to watch me squirm. However, I was determined to foil her this trip by not reacting, so I just evaluated her activities as coolly and as silently as a nurse on a mental ward.

I dreamt of my first English breakfast that night. Breakfast was a curio in my life, gone the way of tin lunchboxes and Frogger. Once an indispensable part of my existence, it had slowly lost relevance. While I wouldn't be opposed to having a breakfast, it wasn't something I'd bother to prepare for myself. But the very name, bed and breakfast, conjured up two of my favorite things: sleep and food.

"Good morning, ladies," John said as my mother and I walked down the stairs into the breakfast room the next morning. My mother surveyed the breakfast bar set against the back wall—a serving bowl full of scab-like prunes in juice, a canister of corn flakes, and a dish of stringy grapefruit quarters.

"I know Ashley's hungry," my mother said, the tone of sarcasm in her voice too subtle for John to catch.

We sat down at the table nearest the window and waited for our coffee. John had asked us what we "desired" for breakfast. I said I'd have the English breakfast. My mother said she'd have a bowl of corn flakes from the breakfast bar. John looked crushed. A few minutes later he emerged from the back kitchen with my first English breakfast balanced on his palm: two slabs of ham, thick and curled around the edges; a soft-boiled egg, the yolk suspended in a delicate skin of egg white; a brown sausage, smooth and taut under its casing; and a fat, midget tomato. It looked like dinner.

My mother watched me as I ate; it was an annoying habit of hers. If she caught one of her daughters (she had three) tucking into a bag of potato chips, she'd say, "Like those chips?" If, on the other hand, we caught her eating a Mal-o-mar in the sunroom while watching *Larry King Live*, she'd stuff the offending wrapper between the sofa cushions before we had a chance to comment. My sisters found such behavior amusing and would often pounce on my mother, laughing, and try to find the wrapper so they could say "Like those Mal-o-mars, Mom?" I, on the other hand, always felt embarrassed when I interrupted my mother's covert snacking, and said nothing. So it was with this history of aggravation that I thought about asking my mother to stop watching me eat. But I hesitated, and during that moment of hesitation, my mother picked up her fork and speared a piece of my ham.

◄ ►

It was cool dusk when my mother and I arrived in Moreton-in-Marsh, a north Cotswold village on the Fosse Way. When we attempted to check in to the Redesdale Arms hotel, no one was at the front desk, and no one appeared after we rang the bell. My mother stomped into the vacant dining room and reappeared with a bartender.

"I'm sorry," he said, tugging at his bowtie, "our front desk help quit this morning." He blinked furiously behind his thick glasses. I found myself trying to lip-read. His thick country accent rendered much of what he said muddy and difficult to decipher. Like she had done on a number of occasions since we had arrived in England, my mother nodded and smiled when she was spoken to, and pretended like she understood what the bartender was saying as he checked us in. My mother thought she could fake it by watching the speaker intently, and look like she was paying attention. When the speaker would stare at her expectantly, waiting for a response or a reaction, she would come up empty. And, instead of asking the person to repeat himself, she'd panic, put her hands to her head and say, "Before I can answer any questions, I have to have my coffee." Most often this response came quite far removed from her morning coffee, and whomever she was speaking to looked doubtful and a little sad.

After the bartender checked us in, we headed to the pub where he was tending the bar and where my mother wanted to down a Guinness or three. Because we were the only patrons in the place, he tossed us a deck of injured poker cards. He watched us struggle to remember the rules of Poker and Blackjack. He seemed decidedly unimpressed when he saw us begin a game of Go Fish.

"Do you have a nine of puppy dog's feet?" Sip of Guinness.

"No clubs, Mom. Go Fish. Do you have the ten of spades?"

"You mean the ten of shovels?"

Sigh.

I had fallen prey to my mother's carefully fashioned eccentricities. For the years that I'd been in my mother's life, she'd been a disheveled, idiosyncratic, self-made caricature of herself. I remember how shocked I was when I stumbled across old wedding photographs tucked away in my mother's underwear drawer. A slim, petite woman with long, smooth black hair pulled away from her face to reveal an attractive, broad forehead, was holding a bouquet of silk gardenias. She was smiling demurely. Her beauty so mesmerized me that I didn't immediately notice that the groom in the photograph was not my father. I learned, after considerable effort, that my mother had married once before. She had kept it a secret for thirteen years. The man in the wedding photographs was an alcoholic ex-soldier named Carl who had an overbite and no decorations. After my discovery, my mother preferred to keep both Carl and his bride tucked away in a box in our attic.

After a restless night at the Redesdale Arms—beds with swayed box springs and itchy sheets—we prepared for a bike tour of the Cotswolds. An unguided bicycle tour of the Cotswolds was ambitious any way you looked at it, but it was especially daring for us because our combined sense of direction was "I still don't understand how to get the needle to go north on this compass!" I was wearing the bike shorts that my mother had so carefully packed for me, folded into a kind of tent thanks to the cardboard crotch protector. It seemed, to my mother, vitally important that we avoid straining that part of our body, where a bike seat can be so cruel.

"How far are we going today?" my mother asked.

I knew the response she was looking for was "Two miles, Mom, then we'll stop for lunch," but I consulted my mental almanac of my father's accomplishments for the appropriate answer. My father was the very model of fitness, climbing Mt. Kilimanjaro and Mt. Rainier in one year, trekking through Peru the next, ice climbing frozen waterfalls and running up hilly jogging trails wearing a forty-pound weight vest.

At the end of our sixteen-mile trek, my mother had conquered a number of Cotswold hills on foot, pushing her bike. We were set for another outing the next day and we looked forward to it. But when we woke up the next morning, we could barely walk. It seems the crotch-protecting bike shorts hadn't done their job. The pain was excruciating, the kind which is impossible to adequately recount to others. I watched my mother walk bow-legged to the bathroom.

"It'll be better once we get on the bike," I said to her through the bathroom door. She walked out with a pair of underwear in her hand (left to dry on the sill overnight) and grimaced. It was a look that said, "Hey kid, I've been there. I've been face to face with the kind of pain you only read about in war novels. This is the front line and if you think you can beat this kind of pain, then you are in for the shock of your life."

One mile into our second bike tour and I was on the front line of physiological warfare. The pain was insidious and embarrassing and shared. My mother and I approached hills bitterly. We felt betrayed by sharp curves. Now my mother pushed her bike whenever she thought I wasn't looking.

That evening my mother and I decided to stuff ourselves at dinner. The cost was absorbed in our bike package, along with the price of the hotel room. Since it was paid for, my mother said, might as well "fill 'er up." I pointed out that we had stuffed ourselves to the point of pain every night since we arrived in England.

"But we don't eat that often," my mother said. "Pass the clotted cream." In the presence of others, both my mother and I ate the way many women do—small, delicate bites, taking care to wipe our mouths, running our tongue over our teeth to be sure nothing has lodged between them. But something strange happens when it's just my mother and I eating; we devour our meal as if it is our last.

"Yes, we don't eat that often, but when we do, we feast," I said. Food was an "issue" in my house. My mother had been watching her weight ever since she'd had children. I, too, had been engaged in a perpetual battle with food. By phone, my mother shared her latest Weight Watchers' success or disappointment, and I told her that I'd finally gotten on a regular exercise regimen. We traded weight loss aphorisms, but when we were away from home, something changed. We ate without hesitation. It was the only time I ever felt comfortable eating around my mother.

"Well, I think we deserve it. We've watched our diet to get in shape for this bike trip and I think we owe it to ourselves to have a dessert one night, or an extra helping of carbohydrates. Will you hand me the butter? No, not that light crap." Rationalization was understandable, but in truth, every meal was another feeding. Dish it up, slop it up, put it on a plate and we'd lick that plate.

◄ ►

We moved on to Stratford-Upon-Avon the next morning, a pretty town where the black timbers of pubs and houses curved under the weight of years and where nearly everything was named after a Shakespeare play. Shakespeare was born here, and though he spent most of his life in London, this town is a proud and somewhat obsessive sycophant.

I knew my mother had recently purchased an electric-powered paper shredder, but I had not foreseen her manic need to shred paper on the road. Tickets, restaurant bills, receipts—receipts were especially frustrating. A single credit card receipt had to be ripped up in intervals and disposed of in at least three different trash cans. My mother thought this ingenious. She carried pocketfuls of shredded paper and sometimes I'd see her put her hand in the pocket and rifle through the scraps before they were distributed in a host of trash cans.

"People dig through trash cans, trying to piece together one single receipt," my mother said when I told her that I'd had a dream of sound the night before—no images, only sound. The sound of paper being torn, shredded, deposited.

"I mean, your life is on that receipt," she said.

"The business doesn't put your whole credit card number on it, Mom." I said.

"No, *they're* sharp. *They* can figure it out."

I imagined a "they" that was proficient at finite mathematics and the laws of probability. I pictured "them" digging through a trash can outside of the train station where we'd just arrived, finding a receipt, scurrying to a nearby doorway, and calculating probability down to the only numbers that could possibly complete my mother's credit card number. This was just one of a host of idiosyncrasies that had grown more and more grating the older she got.

"Just part of getting old," she said when I asked her about it.

Getting old was something my mother seemed to have been doing ever since I could remember. It's not that she looked old—she didn't; and, in fact, she often got unsolicited compliments from strange men. Once, on a New York City subway, a handsome older man with a giant gold-plated crucifix on his chest and pomade in his hair stared at my mother all the way from Times Square to 110th Street. When he finally got off, he leaned close to my mother and told her she was "a very beautiful woman." Incidentally, that same day a man walking the opposite direction on the Broadway called my mother a "hot babe," though I joked that from where I was standing it sounded like "old maid."

But my mother had been getting old by collecting quirks, adding them to her repertoire, and refining them through daily use. Drastic, self-performed haircuts were one thing—once she sheared off so much hair, in an attempt to see what the true color of her hair now was, that she ended up looking like Daddy Warbucks with peach fuzz—wearing her underwear to the point of disintegration was another. She also had taken to passing gas at family gatherings and ending her phone calls by shouting "Cheers!"

At one point, after reading an article about early-onset Alzheimer's in which these peculiarities were considered symptoms, I grew worried. But my mother was more complex, and more lucid, than I gave her credit for. These new habits had been deliberated over and added to her personality only after careful consideration. Her persona was her life's work, in a way that it wasn't for most people. Unusual habits were acquired, given a test-run and, if met with adequate forehead slapping from her daughters, adopted. My mother was almost willfully different from the woman in the wedding photographs I'd stumbled across. She seemed to want to elicit a more complex reaction from people, one composed of both attraction and repulsion. I was beginning to think that my mother wasn't becoming eccentric, but instead was simply leaving the cheerleader and the army wife behind.

The next morning, after waking up in our third bed and breakfast (this one called Eversley Bears, filled with hundreds of teddy bears, and run by a grumpy man named Clive), my mother and I trudged downstairs for breakfast. I'd quickly realized that my mother absolutely refused to try an English breakfast; it was too heavy. Like an idiot, though, I kept trying one every time, hoping that a pan-cake might appear on the plate in place of that slimy ham, or a crisp piece of bacon in the place of the boiled tomato which sat on the plate like a bloody blister. But Clive brought the plate out, set it on the table, and stared at me. I cut into the sausage, which was matte and thick, and the casing resisted the knife. I took a large bite out of the fried bread instead and Clive seemed satisfied.

"You look like one who'd take a big English breakfast each morning," he said. I cringed, and wondered what had given me away as one who inhales sausage, deep fried bread, and eggs each morning. I was trying not to get upset by these side comments anymore; just the day before I'd taken my mother's comment that I needed to watch my diet because of my "peasant build" rather well. I'd spent ten minutes in the bathroom that morning, though, searching for my hump and was happy that I hadn't started dragging my knuckles yet.

After breakfast, I wandered into the hallway and stud-ied the souvenir plates that hung on the walls. Teddy in Paris. Teddy in Edinburgh. Teddy in Wichita, Kansas. Then I noticed a framed black-and-white photograph of a uni-formed Clive, shaking the Pope's hand. The Pope appeared to be looking at the man next to Clive in the reception line. I asked my mother if we could leave for London a day early.

In London, the sky opened and reopened like a wound.

My mother and I were forever ducking into cafes and waiting out sudden rain bursts. One thing that broke my ennui every once in a while was watching my mother dump her clothes in London trash bins. She had been obsessed with lightening her load from the first day we arrived in England, dumping a pair of black pants at the bus station at Heathrow. I felt bad for her as I watched her claw through her clothes, her backpack open on a random bench on a railway platform or on a bus seat. She had gone to so much trouble to pack with NASA-like precision and methodology, and now the inside of her backpack looked like a Salvation Army donation bag. I knew we were getting close to the end of our journey when I saw my mother tie one of her last two pairs of underwear in a knot, and dump it in a trash bin in Russell Square. The salad days of stuffing stray shirts in crevices at railway stations were over. We were down to the bare essentials, and even those were being cast off.

The actions of this woman were hard to reconcile with the stories and photographs of the well-groomed, well-coiffed, and well-mannered office main squeeze with the nice legs and the Irish Setter. I remember how shocked I'd been when my mother told me that she'd once run for Miss Bowling Air Force Base. She'd been one of three finalists. During the interview segment, she'd been asked what American woman she most admired. She said she admired Jacqueline Kennedy for her elegance and grace. At the time, I'm sure that seemed the appropriate answer.

Mom was always the prettiest one at the party. And, she'd hoped her daughters always would be the prettiest ones at the party too, and two of them always were. I, on the other hand, disparaged that hope for many years, told my mother it was shallow and petty. I was conspicuously tomboyish and chronically date-less. I tried very hard to disappoint my mother in her hopes and did my best to let her know that I thought her expectations of me should have been of a sort different from the cheerleader and prom queen variety. Eventually, I wore her down, and she stopped expecting me to be like her in any way. When these expectations disappeared, though, I felt inexpressibly sad.

◄ ►

At dinner the night before we were due home, I asked my mother how she'd liked England.

"Well," she said, thoughtfully, "they're stingy with ice cubes," she said. My mother had brought this qualm up so many times during our trip that I had begun to imagine ice cubes a precious commodity.

"There, next to the Crown Jewels—a single ice cube on display," I said, and my mother laughed.

We arrived at the Underground station in time to catch the last train to Victoria Station. It seemed my mother and I were the only sober people on the platform—and I wasn't so sure about my mother. When we sat down in the subway car, I looked at my mother, her sunglasses hiding her eyes even though it was near midnight, and wondered what she was thinking. I'd often catch my mother looking at me, seeming to study me.

"What?" I'd say.

"Nothing," she'd reply, as if it really had been nothing.

For many years, I'd assumed this clandestine staring was a critical assessment. She always denied that it was, and I never believed her; but now I wonder if it was a way of communicating something that she was afraid to say out loud to me—that she loved me. It was something she didn't say directly to me the way she did to my sisters, to whom she was closer and around whom she felt more comfortable.

"She's afraid of you," my sister Lacy told me once. "Not because you're mean, but because you don't want to be who she is. That's a way of saying the things she values in life are trivial." What I didn't tell my sister was that what she'd said was exactly the way I believed my mother felt about me.

Travel somehow made us seem less frightening to each other. Its fleeting scenes and its ephemeral moments that are of either great consequence, or none at all, meant that little was set in stone. My mother and I get along better because we now think of life as that clichéd journey. Stuck

at home, in the same house, it seemed we were not moving. The longer I lived away from home, the further my mother believes I've journeyed, and the more interesting I seem to her. But the more I get to know my mother, the more I realize that she, too, has traveled. I get the stories in snatches, tossed off as if they are unimportant details. "I was Attorney General Ramsay Clarke's secretary." "I was the main breadwinner for the first five years of our marriage." "The boss took me to strip clubs on my lunch break." Each trip we take together is long-overdue disclosure of secrets and of feelings. When we're at home together, now, we are better able to continue disclosing because we've proven that it can be done, that it needs to be done. The spell of home is still strong, but it's not strong enough to take away what has already been revealed to me by my mother. Understanding who my mother is, who she believes herself to be, is a gift I've received in installments, trip by trip. There are many places yet to visit.

The Day I Met My Mother

RUSTY FISCHER

technically, I'd known my mom for eleven years. But I never really "met" her until the day she told us she was getting a divorce…

It was a sunny day in Florida, the very end of summer. We had just returned from another family vacation—make that our last family vacation—to the mountains of North Carolina, where we'd rented a cabin for two weeks every single summer for as long as I could remember.

Still, even before my mom told us about the divorce, I'd known things were somewhat different that sad and fateful year. For one, we didn't drive up to the mountains. We flew. And not the four of us, like last year and the year before. This time there were only three tickets.

"Your father's very busy this year," my mom said, and my little brother, Rhett, and I looked at each other and shrugged. Dad owned a restaurant in town, and we knew most days were busy. Still, he'd always managed to scrape together two weeks for us in the past. He must have been really busy to miss the beginning of our family vacation…

Then, he didn't join us in North Carolina until the last few days of vacation. He drove up all by himself in our big blue van—we would drive home together as a family, at least—and slept most of the time once he arrived. Mom, Rhett, and I continued playing "three's company" until our vacation was finally over and it was time to drive home.

As usual, Rhett and I played with our Star Wars men on the long back seat of the van while my mom and dad listened to their favorite eight-track cassette in the van's stereo: John Denver singing "Rocky Mountain High," over and over and over again! The only bright spot was the big bucket of Kentucky Fried Chicken we always got as soon as we entered the city limits to Cocoa Beach, our hometown for as long as I could remember.

It was a family tradition, as time honored as it was greasy. Mom would always be too tired to cook after two weeks of eating out and ordering in, and Dad didn't want to go near the restaurant until he'd had a good night's sleep after his long drive home. The solution? Good old KFC! For eight long hours, from North Carolina to the east coast of Central Florida, I'd dreamt of that greasy, crispy, dried-out fried chicken. Not to mention the mashed potatoes, gravy, and biscuits! Mom was a great cook, and never let us have fast food. This was a rare treat we only got to enjoy once a year.

But as we entered the familiar confines of our tiny little beach town and Rhett and I started drooling, Dad drove by the familiar red and white fast food franchise without even pausing.

"Hey," we groaned from the back seat. "What about our chicken?"

Dad mumbled something in reply and Mom, usually our one and only KFC supporter, just sniffled. We knew what that meant. Macaroni and cheese from a box. Oh well, it wasn't fried chicken, but at least it wasn't Brussels sprouts and liver!

When we got home, Dad helped us bring the bags just inside the front door and then made a quick excuse about running back to the restaurant for "an emergency." Before leaving that day, however, he did something very rare indeed: He hugged my little brother and I good-bye. Right there in the driveway, in front of the whole neighborhood!

Mom didn't even bother making us unpack, a chore she usually insisted we complete before the van's engine had even stopped ticking. Instead, she simply told us to get our bathing suits on and meet her in the pool.

Mom was already sitting on the steps in the shallow end, waiting for us. "Sit here with me, boys," she said solemnly, her mood in direct opposition to the bright Florida sun beaming down on the cool, clear water. "I have something I want to tell you."

More quick glances and shoulder shrugs between my brother and I. Inside, I groaned. The last time my mother had said, "I have something I want to tell you," she'd dropped the bomb that I would not be getting the full-scale Millennium Falcon for Christmas!

But what could have possibly gone wrong now?

"There's no easy way to say this," she said simply, her hands trembling as they flitted just above the surface of the crystal clear pool water. "Your father and I are getting a divorce."

Then she started crying. I don't think she really stopped until we went back to school.

Divorce. The word didn't mean a whole lot to me. I knew what it *meant*, of course, and since my mom obviously couldn't speak anymore, I quickly explained what it meant to my little brother. He was curiously quiet, and spent the rest of the afternoon lounging around the shallow end, patting my mother on the back.

Still, I was rather numb. The years of alternating weekends and Dad's bachelor pad, of remarriage and stepbrothers and sisters, of crazy holidays and strained visits were far, far off in the distant future. For the moment, however, I was curiously craving that simple, greasy bucket of fried chicken.

At the time, I assumed I was just hungry and looking for something to take my mind off of my mother's tears. Looking back, however, I think I was more in need of the normalcy that red and white bucket of sizzling drumsticks provided. Its comfort. Its simplicity. If I could have only gone back in time to the summer before, when my parents weren't getting a divorce, or the summer before that, or before that, or even the summer before that...when things were still safe...when things were still normal...when we were still a family.

The sun soon burned our North Carolina skins, and after quick but effective hugs, my mom retired to her bedroom for a much-needed nap. My brother soon tired as well, and fell asleep in his bathrobe on the living room couch, the smell of Solarcaine still lingering around his cherubic little face.

I grabbed a Little Debbie brownie, my favorite, out of my emergency stash in the fridge and found myself wandering around the house, wondering how my dad could leave the place we'd all lived together for all of my eleven years.

Quickly, I began noticing things. Missing things, to be exact. My dad's favorite picture from the living room, for starters. The one with the sailboat and the lighthouse. There was a big square on the wall where it once hung, slightly darker in paint than the faded beige that surrounded it.

His trophies were missing from the den, too. His car wasn't in the garage, sure, I'd seen him drive off in it, but his golf clubs and tennis racket were gone, too. He'd left the tool box, but most of the tools were missing. He'd even taken one of our two matching garbage cans. The big gray ones with the tight rubber lids. I'd helped him pick them out at the hardware store one rare Sunday when he'd had off.

There wasn't much missing in the kitchen, but he'd

taken the poker chips from off the top of the bar and two of the padded barstools. Some of the eight-track tapes were gone, too. More John Denver. Don Ho. Anne Murray. (He never did have good taste in music.) He left all the Christmas albums and the soundtrack to *Gone with the Wind*, my mom's favorite movie. Somehow, I thought, it would have been better if he'd taken it with him, to remember her by.

In the end, it seemed like all he took was *his* stuff. Golf balls. WD-40. Speed Stick. Heineken. Nothing from me. Not my favorite shirt he could maybe smell once a week. Not one of Rhett's chubby teddy bears for old time's sake. Not even one of Mom's prized matchbooks from her collection in the oversized brandy snifter. Didn't he want anything to remember us by? Anything at all?

As I neared my mom's room, I heard her snoring from outside the cracked bedroom door. I crept in, wanting to make sure she was all right. I watched her chest rise once, twice, three times, noticed the mascara on her pillow, then noticed Dad's pillow. Gone. How strange to see only one pillow on your parent's bed.

In the closet, all his clothes were gone as well. Every shirt, every tie, every jacket, every sock. The top of the bureau was two weeks dusty, leaving imprints from where his cologne and change bowl had stood for so many, many years. In the bathroom, two shelves of the medicine cabinet were now free of his Old Spice and Preparation H.

No wonder he hadn't had time to go on vacation with us this year. He'd been too busy moving out. From behind me I heard a sniffle and my mom croaked, "It's all gone."

"Forever?" I asked, looking in the bathroom mirror. I could see her reflection behind me, wiping her eyes. She nodded.

"Forever," she confirmed.

She wasn't angry, yet. That would come later. She wasn't lonely, yet. That would come later, too. For now, she was just plain sad. I turned around and saw her arms open wide, waiting for me. I hugged her, but even at eleven I knew I wasn't the one who needed comforting.

Countless dinners, endless birthday cakes, even more Band-Aids. And my mom had given me each and every one. Without question. Without fail. Without complaint. Now she needed me. For once, I was the only one who could help her. I broke free from her hug and put her back to bed, pulling the covers up to her still quivering chin and waiting until her snuffles ended—and her snoring started.

Then I watched her sleep for a minute or two, perhaps seeing her—my own mother—for the very first time.

That night I made dinner. No macaroni and cheese. The oven was still off-limits. No pizza. I wasn't allowed to go into her purse and Dad had even taken his big purple Crown Royal bag full of quarters. But I could make sandwiches. And ice cream.

It was my first day as man of the house.

It was the first time I ever locked the front door, knowing my dad would not be coming through it late that night after work.

It was the first time I ever gave my little brother a bath.

It was the first time I ever met my own mom. Looked deep into her eyes. Saw her as a person. It would be a long, long road before she was strong enough to be my mother again.

But I could wait. I owed her that much, at least...

A Story of George

C. MARIE FINN

Over and over again, my mother would introduce me to different men. She was a single mother of three children. The man that she had first married, loosely termed my "father," was an abusive drinker. That ended shortly after I was born and she left with her children. The day came that she introduced me to the one man she would love for the rest of her life; the same man that I would love for the rest of my life. This is the story of George.

Being raised in a single parent family wasn't unusual to me. Most of the children in our neighborhoods had only one parent. My dad would often say he was coming to pick me up, only to disappoint me. Even when he showed, he'd take me to the bar. I'd get a few quarters for the music box and a kiddy cocktail, then return home. Technically, I didn't have a father. To be honest, I really didn't mind.

I spent most of my childhood in Kenosha, Wisconsin. I became ambitious physically, but not mentally. I would often hear my mother tell stories about bullies picking on my little brother, and "Chrissy" coming to his rescue. I was always the leader when it came to games. I lived for challenges, and Kenosha had plenty of those. The idea that I couldn't play outside because there might be someone bad lurking around thrilled me.

Then the day came, although I wouldn't know how special it was until much later in life. There he was, in the dining area with my mom. I remember how tall he was and just how handsome he looked. When my mom introduced me to him, I don't remember speaking. To this day, I wish I could have gotten close enough to smell him. It's funny how a person can remember scents from years ago.

"This is George. George, this is Chrissy." My mother and I never talked much. I usually didn't pay attention to men that she would invite me to meet, but this man was so much different. When he said hello to me, I think the earth reversed itself. He was sincere. He looked into my eyes and straight into my heart. If the earth didn't change, my world certainly did.

Days, nights, then weeks passed. All of those included George. George was staying with us now. He made sure that dinner was on time, the kids got tucked in bed, and mom had her own time. George became interested in my school, my friends, our lives. I enjoyed the laugh that he emitted from his belly. He began to eat dinners with us and stay over night. It felt like the most natural circumstance that we had ever been in.

One day, my mom and George were going to the store. They didn't say which one. I asked them to bring me back a Snickers bar as they left. To most people, it might seem like I didn't ask for much. But at six years old, this was the most important treat a person could give me. We were poor and that meant store treats were out of the question. When I asked them to bring me one, that's all I thought about until they arrived home. I grew anxious, my belly ached, and my heart knew it was coming.

I'm not sure how long they were gone, but to me it felt like hours. When I heard the front screen door shut, I didn't run to greet *them* ... I ran to get that Snickers. I looked at them and checked them over really good, searching for my treat. Neither one of them had the one thing that I can ever remember asking for as a child. I thought that they were probably just pulling a prank, so I waited.

"Chrissy, he got you a kite," my mom said. I couldn't believe it. I was hurt and I felt the pain throughout my body. What in the world would I do with a kite? I had never flown a kite before. I didn't know the meaning of this kite, but I knew good and well how I felt about the Snickers.

"You are such a jerk!" I screamed at George. Anger to me was natural and I gave all I had to him. I stormed into the room that my brother and I shared. I slammed the door shut and let the tears fall. The man that had already given me so much couldn't give me the one thing I wanted.

A few minutes later, my mom entered my room. She told me that I was far from spoiled and the way I had behaved was wrong. She said I should apologize to George because I would have fun with that kite. That tore me apart. She should know me better than that. Without the experience of a kite, how could you ever know it would be better than a Snickers bar?

Later that day, George loaded us all into the car—my mom, my brother, George, his three boys, and me. We went to Lake Michigan to fly kites. I was still upset, physically and mentally. That was all about to change.

George helped me get my kite together. It was yellow with different colored stripes. He had to put the string on it so it wouldn't fly away. Once it was connected, he showed me how to get it into the air and keep it there. He left me there to go check on everyone else. I stood there full of pride. Whatever I had been mad about before didn't matter right now. The breeze was cool, the sky was clear, and the lake was calm. My kite continuously tugged at the roll of string in my hands, and with each tug it went a little higher. I stared at it as if it were an angel. Then it left me. The kite reached the end of the string and it flew right into the lake.

This was a tragedy. Everything that I had heard on the radio said that Lake Michigan was a killer. People would drown, animals get eaten, ships would sink, and kites would turn into Kamikazes. The kite was gone and my glory would sink with it. I felt my mouth open slightly as I turned to beg for help, but before I could make a sound, George and his three boys ran toward the lake. The four of them collectively jumped over the rocks and into the lake to rescue my kite. They recovered my flying angel and delivered it to me unharmed. George then explained to me that the kite could only go so far before running out of string. He laughed and I laughed with him.

After our day at the lake, we went for a drive to look at all the beautiful houses that surrounded the area. We all talked about anything and everything that came to mind. Slowly, we made our way back to the apartment. My mom made dinner and the others watched television. I returned to my room. I had something in my head that needed attention. I was an emotional disaster and I knew what I needed to do.

"Dear George, I am sorry. You are not a jerk. I had a lot of fun today and I am so sorry. I love you. Chrissy." I wrote these words on a small, square, pink piece of paper. This was a first for me. I was sorry and ashamed, and I did love this man.

I went into the living room. I crept toward George without saying a word. I handed him my note and went back to my room. I didn't expect him to ever forgive me. Bedtime came, George said nothing about the note, and life went on.

George and my mother married. We bought a house in Kenosha and stayed there for a while. Over the next few years, we had to move several times and ended up in Mauston, Wisconsin, a town much smaller than Kenosha. George purchased a two-acre lot, put up a trailer, and made us a home. We put in a basement, planted trees and a garden, and added additions to both sides of the house. We cut our own wood to heat the house. This was the time in my life that George taught me the significance of a work ethic.

As the years went by, however, something began to change. I hit sixteen like you would hit ground without a parachute. I decided that rules didn't apply to me anymore. George didn't like that I kept my bedroom door shut at night, but I needed privacy. George was on medication; I was on alcohol and drugs. Our attitudes toward each other became strong and negative. I didn't care what he thought and George became distant to us all.

We were all outside the trailer one day during the spring of my sixteenth year. George went to the tool shed and caught up with me. In his hands was a shotgun and he pointed that gun at me, holding it inches from my chest. If he was trying to make a statement, he picked the wrong person. George told me if I were eighteen, he would shoot me, but I just turned my back and walked away. If he was going to shoot, he should just do it. If not, quit wasting my time. George was sick.

A week later, George told my mom to get out, leave everything, and sign for a divorce. She did as she was told. We never discussed what happened with George. We left and never looked back.

Two years passed. We knew that George would eventually be taken by the leukemia that devoured him inside and outside. I changed a lot during those years. I made good friends, good grades, and held jobs alongside of my track and volleyball activities.

One night, I was sleeping in my room when I heard a light tapping on my door. My mom entered with a look on her face that I can't describe, but it filled me with dread. She came to tell me that George had died. He left it in his will for my uncle to be notified first when he passed. Her eyes were filled with tears. She left something on my dresser for me and shut the door on her way out. I sat up on my bed for a few silent minutes. Memories emerged ... and I smiled. I got up to see what my mother had left. I didn't recognize it at first. I picked up the pink slip of paper and read the words:

"Dear George, I am sorry. You are not a jerk. I had a lot of fun today and I am sorry. I love you. Chrissy."

He had kept that note for all those years, through all the happiness and all the anger and everything in between. I cried for all that was lost. The greatest man that I had ever known was gone. I think of George often. When I need guidance, I think of him. When I need strength, I think of him. When I need love, I think of him. George, I am thinking of you now. I love you. Chrissy.

Conversations on the Edge of a Bed

PATTI K. SEE

my mother has taken up residence in my childhood bedroom after half a century in the same room with my father. One afternoon she and I sit on either side of my old bed. Her feet dangle over the edge like a child's. My son Alex plays between us with a tattered bear that was mine and a brother's and a sister's before me.

She tells me, "Your father needs room to spread out after his knee surgery, so I moved into your old room. I'm close to your dad if he needs anything."

"Everyone needs space," I say. "Especially couples." I would never tell her that I haven't made love with my husband for months. The thought of saying those words aloud to my mother—a woman who conceived and nursed eight babies in the same marriage bed—makes me simultaneously cringe and want to roll across my old bed in laughter. I have needs that aren't being met. My husband does not cherish me. Lines I think are so alien to my mother that she has only heard them on TV.

She shifts herself off the bed to a standing position. "I sleep good in here," she says. "Best I've slept in years." At seventy, she finally has a room of her own.

It's hard to be a feminist when your mother is my mother. Or am I feminist because of my traditional Catholic mother? This is a riddle I cannot answer, though I recognize the stories that make us mother and daughter. My livelihood and passion are based on words, yet I have trained myself not to use them with my mother. Or perhaps I felt most connected to my mother when we didn't need words, that silent touch I miss from childhood.

◄ ►

At my mother's urging, the summer I turned fourteen, I made the big move from the bedroom she sleeps in now to one on the second floor. She coaxed me into one of the bedrooms that had been empty for two years since the last of my siblings moved out. "The whole upstairs to yourself," she said. "You'll want space in high school, your own desk and typewriter."

I patched the nail holes and painted the walls myself, hung posters of Tom Selleck, Magic Johnson, and Pope John Paul the second. For the first time in my life everything I'd ever owned was contained in one room, a kind of ownership that took years to find words for.

The first night upstairs, home late that afternoon from an overnight eighth grade graduation party at a local

motel, I lasted about thirty minutes alone. I wasn't scared, just weepy the way children sometimes get the day after slumber parties. I sneaked out of bed and sat on the landing, listening for movement downstairs.

I appeared in the living room beside my mother as she read the newspaper alone on the couch. She didn't look up even as I slipped under her afghan and watched the ten o'clock news against her shoulder.

"When are you going to bed?" I asked.

She finished the paper and said, "Let's go look at your new room."

Upstairs, she sat on my bed admiring the painted walls. Finally she said, "Go to bed, sleepy girl." I shook my head and cried tears too big for a girl about to start high school. I couldn't have told her about breaking into the motel pool or that one girl smuggled in warm beer and it tasted horrible but I drank anyway, and I acted goofy and then wanted to weep. I couldn't verbalize that I no longer fit where I used to fit and high school meant that might get worse. Most days it seemed like everyone knew something that I missed. I didn't say things like that to my mother, still don't.

I said, "I'm afraid." More tears came.

"Why don't I just lay here by you for a while," she said. She pulled back my bedspread. "Just until you fall asleep."

I don't know if she watched me sleep or crept out on tiptoes like she used to when I was five, or if she ever pined for the lost child I was becoming. We didn't have words for that in my family. I do know I was already six inches taller than she was, and I hugged her around the waist with my gangly arms and sobbed. Then I slept.

◄ ►

Months after my father's knees have healed my mother still sleeps a room away from him. I watch her in the kitchen on her tiptoes, reaching for flour on a middle shelf in a kitchen cupboard.

"Your father never said nice things, still won't," she says over her shoulder. "Too much when I lost a hundred pounds, like losing one body, to say I look good?"

This is how my mother talks to me now: telling crucial statements with her back to me a room away.

I nod. I didn't ask to be her confidante, a traitor to my father.

"Compliments aren't everything," I say loudly. She says nothing back to me.

My mother was lovely as a teenager with her mane of curly dark hair and shocking blue eyes, dimples, and racy red lipstick. She married at eighteen, five foot one and ninety pounds, even with my father's arm draped around her. With each child she added fifteen pounds to her petite frame.

I barely remember my mother obese. I see old pictures of her, pre-1972, and recognize her poses, hand on her hip in front of the Christmas tree or familiar tilt of her head in all of the First Communion photos. I do remember the fall I started kindergarten, and she discovered Lucky Strikes and freedom at forty-five. Mostly I recall her gone three nights a week to Weight Watchers meetings, hitching rides with neighborhood women or my sisters on their way to choir or basketball practice. Over the next eighteen months, her size twenty cut itself in half, until I was afraid she might disappear into her nightgown.

Over twenty years later, I was on the cusp of my own internal transformation as I discovered my voice as a writer. One night I stopped at my parents' house to pick up my two-year-old after a graduate class. Alex was asleep in my childhood bed, pillows on either side of him, sweating beneath two blankets. I sat on the bed and fingered the curls on his forehead.

My mother whispered inches from my face in the dim room, "You eating right? Getting enough sleep?"

I translated: *You look rotten.* Another question coming off as insult, or at least how I had grown to read her comments.

I rolled Alex over and pulled him up to me in one tender and familiar motion. "This is just so hard sometimes," I told her. She wrapped the extra blanket over both of us.

"You chose to go back to school," she said, "so do it. Of course it's hard."

I couldn't tell this woman who left school in eighth grade to work in a canning factory, who had her first baby at nineteen and six more by my age, that I was deconstructing Madame Bovary, reading Tillie Olsen every moment Alex was asleep and I wasn't, that I was writing and publishing poetry. That I was doing all of this to be somebody, even if I didn't know who that somebody might be.

"I know," I said. She kissed Alex good-bye.

So do it, I thought all the way home. And I tell myself even six years later, *You want to be a writer, so do it*. I often return to her matter-of-fact wisdom, and each time I temporarily narrow the distance I've made between my mother and me.

A Helping Hand

ANA RASMUSSEN

my mother lies in a fifth floor hospital bed, hooked up to this tube and that. I am in a recliner across the room, reading a magazine, nothing of consequence to occupy my hands. She needs to relieve herself but is too embarrassed to call for the nurse, too imprisoned to help herself. So she decides to risk the asking.

"Honey," she breathes in her so tiny voice, "could you help me with something here?"

"Sure, Mom," I say, nice and easy, careful not to scare her away. Conscious of how rare it is for her to allow me to be generous with her, of how little access she allows to her soft center. "What do you need?"

"Well, I need to go to the bathroom and I can't do it by myself." A transparent catheter runs yellow beneath the bed, making the details of her current request clear, even as it is unspoken.

"Oh, sure. That's easy," I say, closing the magazine, not sure at all if it will be but hoping that we can figure it out. I walk over to the bed side and gather the IV pole and line in my right hand. She offers up her thin arm to me. Slowly, slowly I ease her to the edge, to her feet, onto her pale, weak legs. I take her small weight against my shoulder,

263

along my hip, under my protection. Holding the half-filled urine bag draped over my left arm, I encircle her diminished body. We inch across the few feet of floor into the cold, clinical, square bathroom.

"I'm sorry," she says. "Sorry to ask you to do this."

"It's OK, Mom. This is easy for me."

"Well, it's not for me," she croaks.

"I know," I say. "I know it's hard." I turn her gently around, set her down on the cool, firm seat, make sure the drooping, open-backed gown is not down in the water.

"OK?" I ask.

"OK. Now you go out."

"Are you sure? I don't mind staying," I say.

"No."

"I won't look, Mom. I wouldn't want you to fall off or anything."

"No," she replies, her jaw tight. "I'll be alright. Now go out and close the door. And don't listen. Go back to your reading. I'll call you when I'm finished."

I do what she asks, a little unsure. A little worried if she is safe. A lot touched by her modesty, her propriety, her pride. I take up my magazine and sit quietly in the chair but do not, cannot, read a word.

No sound escapes from the bathroom. Before long, before I get up to check on her, she calls my name, as loud as her emotion-spent voice can muster. I re-cross the room, open the heavy bathroom door, and come to where she sits.

"Flush the toilet please, honey," she says. "I don't want you to see."

"You know, Mom, I think the nurse might want to measure it."

"Oh. Alright. Just help me up, then. But don't look."

"OK," I say. Again I pull her small weight up against my sturdiness, take her firmly in hand, gather up the tubes that are attached to her, slowly creep her over to the bed, ease her onto the bent mattress, and arrange her limp limbs until she is comfortable.

Red-cheeked and panting from the effort, she says, "There's one more thing I need help with."

"OK. What is it?"

"I couldn't clean myself," she says, in the tiniest voice yet. "I was afraid I was going to fall."

"Oh," I say, slow and easy. "What would you like me to do?"

"Can you bring me a warm washrag?"

"Sure, Mom." I walk over to the narrow closet by the door and pull a clean cloth from the shelf. I take it to the sink across from her bed, run warm water over the cloth, and wring it out. "Here you go," I say, putting it in her hand.

"Thank you," she says. "Now turn around, please. I don't want you to see."

I do what I am told. As I turn away I see her hand pull

265

the washcloth under the sheet, out of sight. I look away, look at the wall, look to what will come next.

In time she says, "Alright. I'm finished. You can turn around now." I turn back toward the bed.

"I'm sorry, honey," she murmurs. "So sorry to ask you to do this."

"It's OK, Mom. It's OK." She closes her eyes.

"I'm a mother too, remember?" I offer. "I've changed lots and lots of diapers. I don't mind."

"Well, I do," she says, her voice rising just a little, the cloth and her hand still hidden under the sheet.

I try again. "You know, I've never been very squeamish. Remember how curious I used to be when you took me to the doctor? And I worked in a clinic all those years," I venture, my voice calm and steady.

"Oh, that's right," she responds. "You did work in that clinic. I guess this isn't all that different."

"No, it's not. We're just people, Mom. There's not much that won't wash off."

"Alright, then," she whispers. "But put on a rubber glove."

"What?" I ask, my bare hand already reaching toward the sheet. "A rubber glove? Mom, I don't think you have anything I'm worried about catching."

"A glove, honey," she persists. "I don't want you taking any chances."

I turn back to the sink, pull a startlingly bright purple

latex glove from the box on the overhead shelf, and put it on my right hand.

"OK," I say, extending my sheathed hand toward her, "I'm ready."

"Here, then," she says, her hand moving slowly out from under the sheet, folding the wet cloth neatly over on itself. And then, one last time, "Don't look," she says. "I don't want you to see."

Again I look away and she lays the still-warm cloth on my ridiculously purple palm. I hesitate, my face averted, all my attention on this small weight, until she gives the final directions.

"Now just drop it in the hamper," she tells me. "OK?"

"OK."

"And throw the glove in the trash."

I do.

"And wash your hands."

I rub my unsoiled hands with soap, rinse and dry them slowly, then turn back toward the bed. "Anything else, Mom?" I ask. "Anything else you need?"

"No. I think I'm fine. I think I'll rest for a while now." Her eyes close right away.

"OK," I say, and head back to my chair.

"Honey," she calls, just as I open the magazine.

"Yes, Mom?"

"Thank you. Thank you for taking such good care of me."

"You're welcome, Mom," I say. "I had a good teacher, you know."

A small smile moves across her face as she drifts off into an untroubled sleep.

With My Son Aboard

ROBERT T. RITCHIE

t he droning of the antique Norseman bush plane pre-
cluded conversation and commanded them to drink in
the visual splendor of the lake country below. Bob was
glad, because things had been tense between him and his
dad while they were loading up. His dad bossed him
around about how and when to do a lot of things Bob
understood perfectly well, from quite a few previous trips.
In the past he had always done what he was told and kept
his mouth shut, but this time he ventured to reply when
some of the orders were unnecessary. He had probably
gone a little too far, judging from his dad's mood.

Just before shoving off, his dad barked, "Check to be
sure the canoe is well lashed to the pontoon."

"Dad, you've already told me to do that. I'm not deaf,
you know."

"Don't talk back to me, son," he said in a tone that told
Bob he wasn't kidding.

"Just because you're a teenager now doesn't mean you
can get unruly."

"No sir," was the reply he expected, and he got it.

When the plane sat down at the Canadian border
ranger station, they were met by four rangers who helped

269

them unload. Bob was surprised that they didn't wear uniforms, but dressed much the same as he and his dad, in checkered woolen shirts, heavy-duty khaki pants, and high-top boots. Their clothes had a few patches, but all of the rangers were clean shaven and neat looking. The head man was named Oscar. He asked Bob's dad for some I.D., then sold them their Canadian fishing licenses. He asked where they came from, where they were going, and how long they'd be in Canada.

His dad showed Oscar their intended route on the map Bob had been carrying. They would portage from Bayley Bay to Pike Lake as soon as they were through checking in. They would cross Pike to their next portage that day, into Burke Lake. Burke would take them to a portage leading to Moose Lake. At the far end of Moose was their campsite for the night, a place called Singing Brook, which Oscar said was the best campsite around. He told them that the two lakes were separated by only about fifty feet, with a full four-foot drop in water levels. This resulted in wildly churning rapids and the water "sang" happily.

Their ultimate destination was Lake Agnes, another day, including one long portage. They would camp there and fish for a week before doubling back.

"Seen anybody else going through here recently in our direction?" his dad asked.

"Nope, not for over a week. You'll have it all to yourselves. But you better get yer arses in gear if you want to take any guns or liquor into the park, you know. You're not carrying any are you?"

Bob's dad dug around in the food rucksack and produced a bottle of Jack Daniels, which he handed to Oscar. "Only this," he said. "I'll leave it here with you guys. I'd appreciate it if you'd take a taste or two everyday to make sure it isn't going bad. If you have any doubts at all, use it up before it spoils, OK?" Oscar grinned gratefully.

At Oscar's direction, the three other husky rangers picked up the canoe and all the other gear and carried it across the portage for us, saving us considerable time and sweat. After the rangers had left us alone on the shore of Pike Lake, Dad said, "Darned nice neighbors, these canucks."

"Did they do that because you gave them the whiskey?"

"No, they'd have done it anyway as long as they had the time. They're that kind of people."

Bob helped load the canoe. This was a very careful operation, since they had a lot of gear to put in a small space and it had to be arranged just so, taking weight distribution into account. Before they shoved off, his dad pointed to an empty space in the middle of the loaded canoe. He said, "You'll sit here instead of up on the front seat, in the stretches where we use the motor, like this first one. You remember why?"

"So we'll have a lower center of gravity and be less

likely to tip," Bob had answered, taking care not to sound smart-ass, but rolling his eyes when he was sure his dad couldn't see his face. He had heard often enough that his dad's goal was to make him self-reliant. Bob believed this and knew there were good reasons for everything they were doing, so he had been learning them well. Did his dad even notice that that he never screwed up seriously?

As they were motoring across Pike Lake, Bob studied the map. Navigating these lakes was not easy, because the shorelines have a way of looking the same everywhere you go...tall pine trees among granite boulders, and no high hills. It helped when there were irregularities in the shore-line, like little bays, or the occasional waterfall marking the entrance of a small stream into the lake. The little islands that dotted the lakes were good landmarks, but you had to keep constant track of which islands you had passed and which ones were still ahead. The trip back was always much easier, his dad had taught him, if you kept your eyes open on the way out for other landmarks. You should always look back at them, over your shoulder, so you'd know what they would look like when you were coming from the other direction. And, of course, you should keep a record of about how long it took to travel each leg of your journey.

After they had been on the water about a half hour, Bob saw the tiny sand beach that marked the beginning of their portage, but he didn't say anything until a couple of minutes later when his dad slowed to an idle and asked him for another look at the map. "I think you passed it," Bob said. His dad simply snorted, revved up the engine again, and kept going in the same direction for another few minutes before stopping for another map check.

"There's supposed to be a little sand beach. Have you seen one?" his dad asked.

"I think we passed it just before that last place you stopped," said Bob respectfully. He didn't *think* so; he knew darned well, but he had to be careful not to sound like he was sassing.

His dad wheeled sharply about and steered a reverse course. When they got near, Bob pointed toward the little sand beach. It was a couple of hundred yards distant and not more than eight or ten feet wide.

"You were right, hotshot," his dad said. "Maybe your gonna be worth your salt on this trip."

Only *maybe*, Bob thought.

Another day and a half of hard work for both of them, with Bob being continually tested by his dad, brought them to the shores of Lake Agnes, where they would strike camp and fish for a few days. Bob set down his burdens and headed for the water to splash a little on his face.

It was about two o'clock. They planned to motor for a couple more hours, then fish maybe two more, 'till time to set up camp and make dinner. Lake Agnes was about fifteen miles long, running north and south, more or less, and the first stretch of water they were to traverse was long enough to allow the north wind to cause fairly large waves to develop. They wouldn't be able to make very good time steering straight into them. So, they decided to troll now for lake trout, as long as they had to go slow anyway.

Bob hooked what felt like a whopper and fought with it about twenty minutes before getting it to the surface and close enough for his dad to grab by the gills and haul aboard. They had no scale, but his dad guessed about eighteen pounds.

"Here, hold him a minute while I take a picture," said his dad. "Then throw him back." We won't be able to eat that much fish before it spoils, and it would be wrong to waste such a fine creature."

Instead they got busy and caught a couple of small walleyes before selecting a pretty little island and found a campsite at its south end. It had a very large granite promontory at its north end, blunting the force of the northerly wind, which had been gaining in strength all afternoon.

As soon as they hefted their gear ashore, his dad asked Bob to pitch their tent, pump up the mattresses, and build a rock fireplace while he took the axe and went after some firewood. It was about five o'clock, and Bob was hungry. He could still hear his dad chopping when he finished his assigned chores, so he decided to show him how well he could clean and filet their catch, as a surprise. He was doing this at the water's edge when he heard a loud cry from his dad, followed by silence.

"Dad! Dad! Are you OK?" Bob shouted, but his dad didn't answer. He left the fish on the rocks at the shoreline and ran in the direction his dad had gone, shouting, "Dad...Where are you?"

A weak voice answered, "This way son. I'm going to need some help."

Bob found him sitting on the ground, looking pale and sweating. "Its my right foot, or ankle, or both. Something's broken. I can't put any weight on it. I'll need your shoulder."

Alarmed, Bob squatted down next to him. Before leaning on his son's shoulder, his dad told him, "Pick up the axe now; you won't be able to after I'm leaning on you. Never lose your axe when you're in the woods."

Bob obeyed. Then, when his dad's arm was around his shoulder, he rose to a vertical position, remembering to keep his back straight and use his legs, while his dad pushed up with his good leg at the same time. They began to make their way back to the campsite very slowly, one carefully placed step at a time.

"What happened, Dad?"

"Stupid thing. Didn't look where I was putting my foot while I was rolling the trunk of the fallen tree I was working on. Stepped in a crack in the rocks, lost my footing, and fell sideways." His dad had grunted in pain between words as he spoke.

When they got back, Bob managed to get him into the tent on one mattress, in a sitting position, with the other mattress folded in half behind him to lean on. "Take off the boot and the sock," he was told. "Thank God," said his dad, "No flesh broken." His foot and ankle were badly discolored, however, and swelling fast. "Pail of cold water," said his dad. "Soak it a while."

A few minutes later, "Get me the aspirin from the first aid kit, and find the other whiskey bottle I snuck past Oscar." Bob did so, and his dad took a long pull on the whiskey bottle and swallowed a few aspirin.

By now, it was almost dark, but the wind hadn't let up much. It whistled eerily through the trees. But the sky was still clear. His dad looked up. "Think it will rain very soon son?"

"Not before tomorrow," Bob answered.

"Good. That'll make it easier for you. Easier to do what you've got to do. I'm out of action. You take over." He sounded pretty groggy, and he looked like hell. "I'm going to lie down now," he said. He was out cold right away.

Bob took the water bucket and set it aside. He unzipped both sleeping bags, put one of them over his dad as a blanket, and left the other one within reach. Then he went back to the lake to fill two more cooking pails with water, which he also put near his dad. From the food sack, he removed as many cans of corned beef, Spam, baked beans, corn, and evaporated milk as he could find and placed them next to the water pails, along with the can opener, some utensils, and the small flashlight.

He built a good fire and let it quiet down past the roaring stage before he piled on several more logs. Bob used the damper wood, which wouldn't burn so fast, because he wanted a fire that would burn through the night, to discourage bears and wolves from wandering into the campsite, even though he doubted there were any on such a small island. That was one of the reasons for camping there, after all. He hoped the north wind wouldn't shift and blow the smoke toward the tent.

Thankfully, there was already some chopped wood at their campsite, left by the last group who had used the little island. The reason for that tradition seemed more obvious now. He wouldn't have time now to chop any more. Maybe he'd have time when he came back later.

Having put everything they had within reach of his dad, he set about preparing to get back to the ranger station for help. The motor was still on the canoe. They had only used part of a five gallon fuel can. Good. He would take a full one and that would be plenty. He'd take both paddles, since he'd need them for a yoke to carry the canoe. What else might he need? His warm jacket, mosquito dope, the axe, a few candy bars, a drinking cup, some rope, a spare spark plug and cotter pin for the engine's prop from the tackle box, and hand tools. He checked that his hunting knife was still on his belt.

Anything else? The map! The large flashlight! Oh yeah, and matches. And the compass, just in case he lost his way. He emptied the clothing rucksack and put everything but the gas can inside it to keep things dry. The few things he was taking barely covered the bottom of the sack.

Whoops, the bacon and lard. Can't leave them in the tent with dad. Bob sealed them both tight and hauled them up into a tree.

The canoe would ride too low at the stern with just him in it, so he extended the motor tiller using a small birch branch and some duct tape. That way he could ride on his knees, rather forward, and still steer alright. He also put a couple of large rocks in the bow for ballast.

That was it. All he could think of. It was already nine o'clock. Time to get moving. He poked the fire and added a log. Then he checked on his dad, who was lying flat on his back, breathing heavily. He felt his forehead. It was hot, and that scared him.

"Dad," he said hoarsely, "I'm going now."

His dad didn't open his eyes or say anything, but Bob saw him nod slightly and raise his hand an inch or two, just for a moment.

◄ ►

As he was racing south on Lake Agnes toward the long portage to Sunday Lake, Bob recalled how long they had spent on each leg of their inbound trip. Making allowances for the time they'd spent fishing and having meals, and considering that he had the wind with him instead of against him, Bob figured that, with luck, he would need a little over seven hours. Call it eight. His goal was to make the ranger station by five in the morning.

The big obstacle was the first long "killer" portage. He had no trouble finding it, since he had kept his eyes open on their way outbound and since there was moonlight to help...and starlight, millions and millions of stars in the crystal clear sky. The moon and stars helped him on the water, but when he dragged the canoe ashore at the start of the portage, he found that the dense pine forest immediately blacked out practically all light from above.

His dad was hurting, so he had no time to waste. Bob immediately unloaded the aluminum canoe. Then he found an approximately horizontal pine branch about five feet above the ground, close by. With the axe, he quickly stripped it of its smaller branches, twigs, and pinecones. Now came one of the tougher tasks. He had to get the canoe in a position that would let him step under the middle before accepting its weight on his shoulders. First he lashed the paddles into a yoke. Then he had to drag the canoe under the branch, flip it upside down, and lift the bow up to rest on it. Now he could squeeze in under the yoke.

He would have to make two trips. He decided to leave the canoe resting on its branch for now, and make the easier trip first, carrying the lightly loaded rucksack with the axe strapped to it, the motor, and the five gallon gas can. With duct tape, he strapped the flashlight to the handle of the gas can, so that he could point it ahead and control the direction of its beam to a degree as he walked.

Off he went. He had done this before with practically the same load, so he knew he could handle it. What he didn't know was how hard it was in the dark, even with a flashlight, to find secure places to put his feet so that he wouldn't lose his footing and drop the motor. He couldn't afford to step on loose stones or muddy places. One broken bone in the family was enough for now, thank you. It was extremely slow going.

As he trudged across the portage, there was complete silence, most of the time. The angry sounding whine of mosquitoes patrolling around his neck and ears was a frequent and unwelcome exception. His hands weren't free to slap at them, so he was glad he was well smeared with citronella.

Every now and then he heard rustling in the underbrush. It sounded like ten or twenty yards off the trail. He figured it was the sound of some kind of animal, keeping up with him. Deer, moose, porcupine, bear, wolf? Most likely bear or wolf, he thought. The others would try to avoid him rather than follow. But he felt sure he was safe. It was midsummer and the animals had plenty to eat. He wasn't carrying any raw food. He knew they wouldn't attack. Maybe they could smell from his hands the fish that he had been cleaning when his dad had been hurt. Most likely they were just curious. He struggled on.

When at last he reached the Sunday Lake side of the portage, it was nearly four o'clock. With another trip to make, he'd never get to the ranger station by sun-up. He would have to jog instead of walk back.

The second trip with the canoe was more difficult. He found he needed to rest frequently by letting the stern down to the ground and just standing still, bearing only part of the weight, for a few minutes, to catch his breath. A few times he found convenient low branches on which to rest the bow, getting out from under the load entirely long enough to rub his sore neck, shoulder and back muscles, and to stretch the kinks. He wanted to get there fast, but the important thing was to get there, so he didn't press himself so hard that he might risk an injury. He took every step carefully. A foot could slip a little on a spot of gravel, so he concentrated on keeping his balance.

He kept his mind on the remainder of the trip, which would be a piece of cake by comparison. Bob looked up at the sky. Fog was setting in so that he couldn't see the moon and the stars anymore. He was glad that all he had to do at Singing Brook was drag the canoe a few yards to Moose, so he wouldn't even have to unload it. The portage from Moose to Pike would be medium-tough, but at the last portage to the ranger station, he would simply leave everything and run across.

It was about five forty in the morning when Bob came puffing up to the kitchen door of the rangers' main lodge. Oscar was stirring what looked like pancake batter while a huge pot of coffee was brewing on their kerosene stove. Between gasps for air, Bob blurted out, "My dad is hurt. Can't walk. Fever. Broken ankle, we think. Real swollen. Lake Agnes, on an island a few miles into the main body of the lake."

"We'll get a seaplane to take him to the Ely hospital," said Oscar, who went immediately to a radio console in the corner of the room, static crackling softly from its speaker.

"Bob, you look like you could use some coffee, right?" asked Oscar. Actually, Bob hadn't started drinking coffee yet, but it seemed like a helluva good idea. He gave Oscar an affirmative nod.

"Couple of pancakes?"

"Yes. Please." Bob ate ravenously.

"When you're through, you can rest a bit on the spare bunk in that corner, eh? You'll hear the plane when it gets here."

The roar of the little bush plane's engine as it taxied to the rangers' dock woke Bob from his short but sound sleep. He was instantly on his feet and running to meet it. The fog had lifted to perhaps two or three hundred feet above the tree level.

282

"Hop right in," shouted the pilot, a big hulk of a redhead with a full beard. As Bob did, he noticed a perforated aluminum litter strapped on the pontoon struts on the passenger side. "No time to lose with this changing weather," the pilot continued. "Flying blind's not a good idea around here. Got your map?" Bob nodded as Oscar was pushing the plane away from the dock.

When they were airborne, the pilot leaned over and shouted, "I'm Rusty, who're you?" Bob said his name and they shook hands. Rusty had a very strong grip, but Bob felt he matched it nearly enough.

"And your partner's name?"

"Dad...'er, Jack."

"He much bigger'n you?"

"Yeah, but he's smaller than you."

"Guess the two of us can handle him OK, then."

"Yep. He's got one good leg, too, and he's pretty strong," said Bob.

Rusty grinned and said, "How about showing me where your partner's at on Lake Agnes?" Bob showed him the little island on the map. "Camped at the south end?" Another nod from Bob. "Good. Winds still out of the north. We can land straight into it and taxi right up to your campsite. Be there in a few minutes."

The few miles that had taken so many hours by canoe and on foot were quickly eaten up and Bob found himself skipping along the tops of the waves straight at their little island. When they were very close, Rusty made a U-turn and coasted as close as he could to the rocky shoreline.

"Behind you," said Rusty. Bob looked over his shoulder to see several coils of rope. "Take two of 'em and tie them from the pontoon struts to the nearest trees ashore, one line forward and one aft." Bob thought his dad would have told him what kind of knots to tie, but Rusty didn't.

"Now unstrap that litter and take it up to the tent for your...for Jack, "Rusty hollered. "But wait for me to help you get him in it."

Bob ran to the tent. His dad was lying flat on his back with his eyes closed, but somehow he'd gotten the sleeping bags rolled up and the loose gear stuffed into the big rucksack, except for the water pail.

His dad opened his eyes, which were bright red and swollen. "Time?" he asked Bob.

"Yeah, Dad. How you doing?"

"All the better for seeing you," he croaked, letting his eyes close again.

Bob picked up the water pail and dashed the remains on the embers of their campfire, then took it and the rucksack down to the plane.

Rusty arrived at the tent carrying a fur-lined parka. "Hands over your head, Jack." He pulled the parka on him, including the hood over his head. "Going to be a little cold up there."

"Don't need this," said his dad, gesturing toward the

litter. "We can get me in the cabin."

"No way, Jack," answered Rusty. "Too crowded, and a couple of tight corners to get you around. There's hardly any leg room anyway, and to get at it, we'd have to twist that leg too much. Now, lie down on your good side."

"You haven't got any morphine, have you?"

"Not qualified to dispense it. Hold out for another forty minutes or so." His dad grimaced.

Rusty and Bob rolled his dad from his side gently into the litter. "Put your arms at your sides, Jack," said Rusty, carefully wrapping a blanket around Jack's legs and feet. Then, he tightened three straps, at the shins, the waist, and chest.

"Talk about helpless," grumbled his dad.

"You've *got* help, Jack," said Rusty.

They hoisted the litter and walked him down to the plane, wading the last few steps since the plane couldn't pull right up to the rocky shore. After placing the litter on the pontoon, with his dad's head forward, Rusty said, "I'll lash him to the plane. You go get the tent and anything loose that's still lying around."

"Will I have to chop any wood?"

Rusty smiled and smacked him on the shoulder. "Not this time, pal, but I'll radio Oscar. One of his rangers will be glad to stop by and take care of it."

285

◄ ►

The flight to Ely took about a half hour. Rusty landed the

little bush plane like he was setting it on cotton candy, he didn't want to dent. There was an ambulance at the dock with two paramedics who took charge of unloading Bob's dad. They were carrying the litter to the ambulance, with Rusty walking alongside. "A little nervous out on that pontoon, Jack?"

"Are you kidding? With my son aboard? If you'd started screwing anything up, he would've figured out how to take over without you."

Bob's chest swelled with pride. *Maybe I could have*, he thought. As they were sliding him into the ambulance, his dad barked out, "Did you remember to douse the fire?"

Bob was surprised to find himself smiling. He looked away from his dad and rolled his eyes. Rusty laughed out loud.

Naming

ELISE GEITHER

my husband is sleeping upstairs with the baby on his chest. I am downstairs playing with her crayons, try-ing unsuccessfully to make the colors blend, when I realize I have never known my grandmother's real name. Coming here, to America, Golden Mountain, Streets of Gold, Rivers of Wine, her name was already changed from the-name-I-never-knew to Mimi, nickname Mims.

She'd always told us the story of how she had been named after her sister who'd died of the coughing. She said she couldn't stand the name, the ghost of the dead girl in the corner of her room at night, in closets, in the pantry eating sweets. My grandmother couldn't hold the name, couldn't tuck it up and under her ribs. It wasn't her. It wasn't hers. So somehow she changed it to Mimi—and this name she held in the market, where she couldn't find potatoes and couldn't speak enough English to ask; in her first home, where she chased out the snakes she said the gypsies had left; over the fire, as she burned all the love letters from her dead husband; over the lake, behind the house he'd built for her.

My mother named me for a princess who had brothers with wings. This princess knit fabrics from nettles, making peace with the poisoned juices as they slid through her fingers. I'd never be that strong, I thought, to knit with a burning flower.

One day, I asked my mother, "What was Oma's name, her real, true name?"

She paused for a moment, looked at the sky and then back at me.

"I think," she said, "it was your name. Yes, it was yours."

I was shocked at first, noticed I was holding my breath. My mother smiled and touched my cheek. She had taken the name, the one full of ghosts and memories and bags of kindling. She had taken that name and with her sore, cricked hands she bent it like a willow, pulled it like pink taffy, and gave it to me. She was strong enough to do this, and then gentle enough to rub my cheek and tickle my back.

My husband is sleeping upstairs with the baby on his chest—the baby I've named with a name too long for her small, pixie chin, fuzzy-chick hair, plump toddling legs. I've given her one name she can hold from Fuling, China, given because she'd been found in the early, frosty morning. And I gave her another name, a name from my mother's favorite movie, to tell her that she can change her name at any time, and I will still know her, find her, sleeping on her father's chest.

Contributor Biographies

OPAL PALMER ADISA is a literary critic, poet, storyteller, artist, and mother of three. She lives in Oakland but remains close to her mother who still lives in Jamaica. They visit yearly and talk weekly. "There is Always a Way," is one of many stories she has written celebrating her love and connection with her mother. Her other published works include the following: two poetry/jazz CD's recorded with Devorah Major, *Fierce/Love* (1992), and *The Tongue Is a Drum* (2002); *Leaf-of-Life*, poetry (Jukebox Press, 2000); *Tamarind and Mango Women*, poetry (1992), PEN Oakland/ Josephine Miles Award Winner; *It Begins With Tears*, novel, (Heinemann, 1997); *traveling women* (1989); *Bake-Face and Other Guava Stories* (1986); and *Pina, The Many-Eyed Fruit*, children's book (1985).

SHARON BRAY writes and works in Silicon Valley, California. Under the name of Wellspring Writers, she leads a variety of creative writing workshops throughout the Bay Area. She has written and published poetry (most recently in *Moxie Magazine*), a number of articles, and a children's book. She is currently completing a book, *Stories of the Journey*, about the healing power of writing for breast cancer survivors, which will be published in 2004 by Amherst Writers and Artists Press. Sharon has a doctorate in applied psychology from the University of Toronto and has completed the Writers Program in Literary Fiction at the University of Washington. She is a senior partner of the Amherst Writers and Artists, Amherst, MA.

LAURA DAVIS is the author of *I Thought We'd Never Speak Again: The Road from Estrangement to Reconciliation*, *The Courage to Heal Workbook*, and *Allies in Healing*. She is the co-author of *The Courage to Heal*, *Beginning to Heal*, and *Becoming the Parent You Want to Be*. Her books have been translated into eleven languages and sold 1.8 million copies worldwide. Ms. Davis lectures and leads workshops on reconciliation nationwide. She facilitates worldwide teleclasses, teaching her students the basic skills of reconciliation. To find out more about her books, lectures, teleclasses, and workshops, or to get a free "Am I Ready to Reconcile?" workbook, go to www.LauraDavis.net.

MARSHA DUBROW earned an MFA in Fiction Writing and Literature at Bennington College, where her chapbook, *Single Blessedness*, was published. She also studied fiction as a Jenny McKean Moore fellow at George Washington University in Washington, DC, and at the University of Iowa Writers' Workshop. Her fiction has appeared in the University of Chicago's *The Awakenings Review*. Her essay, "Gray Matters," is to appear in an anthology entitled *New Aging Women*, and her memoir, "That's All Right Mama" was published in *The Chrysalis Reader*. Her work has run on the covers of *New York* and Britain's *Punch* magazine and its annual book, *Pick of Punch*. She has been a correspondent for *Reuter's* news agency, *Life*, and *People*.

C. MARIE FINN was born in 1971 to Joseph and Carolyn Yancey in Kenosha, WI. She graduated from high school in Mauston, Wisconsin. Her studies consisted mainly of music and arts. Eventually, home became Janesville, Wisconsin. Currently, she is raising her daughters and concentrating on writing for children. She enjoys traveling, writing, her children, her sweetheart, and a variety of sports. She dreams of becoming a successful writer and moving out West.

RUSTY FISCHER has written over thirty books for such reputable publishers as McGraw-Hill, Lebhar-Friedman Books, Mason Crest Publishers, and Frank Schaffer Publications. Over 100 of his essays, stories, tips, and ideas have appeared in such nationally recognized periodicals as *Good Housekeeping*, *Better Homes & Gardens*, and *Seventeen Magazine*. His stories have been anthologized in such bestsellers as *Chicken Soup for the Soul* (HCI), *A Cup of Comfort* (Adams Media), *A Gift of Miracles* (HarperCollins), *The Heart of a Father* (Bethany House), and *God Allows U-turns* (Barbour Publishing). He lives in Orlando, Florida with his beautiful wife Martha and still enjoys a good swim with his mom.

COOPER GALLEGOS was born in Los Angeles into a disjointed, creative family. He wrote his first book when he was six years old. He went to college for twenty years and as a single parent raised two sons on a dirt road in the Mojave Desert. He now lives on the Central Coast of California with his partner of twenty-three years and commutes 140 miles round trip to work. He looks forward to retirement when, he says, "I plan to focus on my writing and teaching myself to ride my bike with no hands."

ELISE GEITHER is mother to Chloe De Chen, adopted from Fuling, China, in November 2002. Life has never been richer or more colorful! Geither's poetry and short stories have been published in *The Artful Dodge*, *The Blue Review*, *Slant*, *The Fossil Record*, *Prose Ax*, and *Morpo* among others. Her short plays have received production in New York and Los Angeles, and her full-length play, *The Doe*, received a staged reading at Weathervane Theatre directed by Michael C. Mazur. Geither teaches English at Baldwin-Wallace College and looks forward to many more adventures with Chloe!

DAVID GOGUEN is a published writer and poet. He has also worked as a writer for newspaper, magazine, radio, and television. He holds an MFA in creative writing from Minnesota State University and currently teaches in the communication arts department at Wilmington College, Ohio.

CHERIE JONES is a twenty-eight-year old mother of two, a writer, and a practicing lawyer. In 1999 she won the Commonwealth Broadcasting Association's Short Story Competition for her short story, "Bride." Her story, "A Day of Deliverance," was a winner in the 1992 First Ladies of the Americas Creative Writing Competition, and won the prize for the best story reflecting the influence of the Caribbean woman on the family. Her stories have been variously published in *Commonwealth Currents* and other magazines. Her non-fiction has appeared in *Island Life* and *MACO Caribbean Lifestyle* magazines. Cherie is currently working on her second collection of short stories. Her first, entitled *The Burning Bush Women and Other Stories*, is slated for publication by Peepal Tree Press in May 2004.

PIROOZ M. KALAYEH is a recent MFA graduate of the Jack Kerouac School of Disembodied Poetics. His stories and poems have appeared in *Nervelantern, 3:2, Yah Boogah Books*, and *Renaissance*. He is currently working on a novel, *The Whopper Strategies*, along with a collection of short stories. He resides in Boulder, Colorado.

RUTH NAYLOR was raised in the contemplative Quaker tradition and graduated from Olney Friends Boarding School prior to attending Bluffton College and later earning a Master's Degree from Bowling Green State University. She married a General Conference Mennonite, taught secondary

English for thirteen years, and then later was ordained and served in the Mennonite Church. Over one hundred of her poems and articles have appeared in publications representing a wide variety of denominations. In her retirement, she is pursuing her writing interests and continues to serve as a spiritual director, having completed specialized training at the Shalem Institute for Spiritual Guidance.

C. A. PECK's first degree(her first love), was in English literature. Somehow along the way she became a chiropractor and an acupuncturist who speaks Japanese, climbs rock faces and plays piano. Everything in her life is constantly changing but the two practices she has held onto for as long as she can remember are running and drinking tea. Born in Scotland and raised mainly in Toronto she now lives in northern California which is all a surprise to her.

MITALI PERKINS was born in Kolkata, India. Her family immigrated first to New York City and then to the San Francisco Bay Area, where Mitali attended junior high and high school. She studied political science at Stanford University and public policy at the University of California, Berkeley. Dedicated to creating and encouraging fiction for young people "caught between cultures," Mitali maintains a Web site entitled "The Fire Escape: Books For and About Young Immigrants" (http://www.mitaliperkins.com). She has written two novels for young readers: *Sunita!* (Little Brown) and *Monsoon Summer* (Random House).

ANA RASMUSSEN—The experiences which led to Ana Rasmussen's story, "A Helping Hand," occurred during a life-and-death week in the hospital with her mother a few years ago. Happily, her mother survived, and their relationship was greatly deepened through their shared experiences. Ana lives in Santa Cruz, California, with her two teenage sons and her new husband. She finds meaningful work as a school counselor but wishes she could devote more time to writing.

PETER REESE is a physician and writer in Boston. He writes for the *Boston Globe Magazine*, and has been published in *The New York Quarterly*. He has read some of his stories on WJHU, the Baltimore/WA affiliate of NPR. He says he is hoping the stripers will keep running thick off Cape Cod this summer.

ROBERT T. RITCHIE was raised in the Chicago area, attended Princeton, and graduated magna cum laude and Phi Beta Kappa. He was a naval officer for three years before entering the marketing research business in which he rose through the ranks to become a senior officer and a director of one of the nation's leading firms. He has a son 42, a daughter 39 (and counting), and four grandchildren.

Recreational passions have included sailing, flying, and scuba. He resides in Sausalito, California.

NANCY ROBERTSON is a writer who lives and works seasonally in Prince Rupert, British Columbia. In the winter she is a "snowbird" who travels to Southern California, Arizona, and Baja. Her writing has appeared in a wide variety of publications including *Prairie Fire* and *Room of One's Own*. Her stories have also been published in the anthologies, *Gifts of Our Fathers* (The Crossing Press, 1994), *Grow Old Along With Me* (Papier-Mache, 1996), and *Creekstones* (Creekston Press, 2000.)

JENNIFER ROBINSON graduated from California State University, Northridge, in 1997 with a bachelor's degree in journalism. Since then, she has written professionally, with stories and articles published in *The Readerville Journal*, *Writers Monthly*, *Full Circle*, *A Journal of Poetry and Prose*, *The Artemis Journal*, *The Acorn Newspaper*, *Riot Brain Magazine*, *The Daily Sundial*, *Living Well Magazine*, and *Bowling Industry Magazine*. She has taken creative writing courses through the UCLA writing program, and received the Los Angeles Daily News Award for "Excellence in Writing." Her book of interrelated short stories, *Tangents*, is currently being reviewed for publication. She lives in Southern California with her husband, and can be reached via e-mail at leslie.robinson14@verizon.net.

MELISSA SANDERS-SELF is a writer and a noted filmmaker. Her documentary, "Writing Women's Lives," aired on PBS. Her first novel, *All That Lives*, was published by Warner Books in 2002, and her short stories have appeared in several anthologies. She was awarded artist residencies at the Djerassi Foundation and the Ucross Foundation, and she is included in Who's Who of American Women and Contemporary Authors for her significant contributions to her field. She currently lives in California and is at work on her second novel.

PATTI K. SEE's work has appeared in *Salon Magazine*, *Women's Studies Quarterly*, *Journal of Developmental Education*, *The Wisconsin Academy Review*, *The Southwest Review*, as well as many other magazines and anthologies. Her book, *Higher Learning: Reading and Writing About College*, a collection of both college and coming-of-age literature, co-authored with Bruce Taylor, was published in the spring of 2000 by Prentice Hall.

ASHLEY SHELBY received an MFA in Nonfiction Writing from Columbia University. Her essays and short stories have appeared in journals like *Post Road*, *Gastronomica*, *The Sonora Review*, *collectedstories.com*, *Small Spiral Notebook*, and *Carve*. Borealis Books will publish her first book, *Red River Rising*, in the spring of 2004. She is currently the co-curator of KGB Bar's Nonfiction Reading Series in New York City's East Village.

LEONIE SHERMAN—*My daughter, Leonie Sherman, is a nomad soul who recently alighted in Haines, Alaska, and a fishing village perched on the edge of the largest protected wilderness area on the planet. At the age of twenty she graduated with honors from the University of Chicago (in less than three years) and has proceeded to forge her own path through the mysterious jungle of life. I am forever grateful that she invited her younger sister and I to join her in protesting the WTO in Seattle where, linked arm in arm, we withstood tear gas, pepper spray, and rubber bullets. Leonie has traveled extensively throughout Southeast Asia, the South Pacific, India, and Nepal and introduced me to the beauties of the Nepali culture and land in the winter of 2000. She teaches women's self-defense, leads bicycle tours, acts as a naturalist, works with emotionally disturbed children and adults, and occasionally fills in for the News Director at the local radio station. She is not only my beloved daughter but also one of my greatest teachers.*

CARYL K. SILLS is currently the chair of the English department at Monmouth University in New Jersey where she teaches both composition and literature. She writes stories about people she knows or just imagines, and in this way, shares with her students an understanding of both the difficulties and rewards of writing. Her leisure times are spent cross-country skiing, playing tennis, and relaxing with her family and their two spirited fox terriers.

TOM SKIERKA studied communications at Eastern

Washington University. He has a background working as an assistant producer for Pinnacle Productions, and later became a columnist for the magazine, *Spokane Woman*. He worked as sports and features editor for *The Valley News Herald*, and developed his own column, "Writing the Pine," which won the Washington Newspaper Press Association's (WNPA) Award for "Best Humorous Column for 1997." The next year, his story "The Tyree Express," featured in *Northwest Indlander Magazine*, was named best sports feature by the Society of Professional Journalists (SPI). That same year, he was hired by the *Spokesman-Review* to cover sports, entertainment, and features. He was a columnist for *Home Notes*, and started the *Idaho Handle Extra* edition of "Where Are They Now?" He continues to write for the *Spokesman-Review*.

CURTIS SMITH has published over two dozen short stories in literary journals such as *Antietam Review, American Literary Review, Greensboro Review, Passages North, South Branch Dakota Review, West*, and *William and Mary Review*. Two stories have been nominated for Pushcarts, and one was named to the BASS Distinguished Stories List. Four of his stories have been accepted for inclusion in other anthologies. His first collection of short stories was *Placing Ourselves Among the Living*. His first novel, *An Unadorned Life*, is due out this spring (Neshui Press). His story, "Have You Seen My Mother, Delilah Bendin?" originally appeared in *Mid-*

299

American Review and will also appear in the upcoming collection of Curtis' stories, *In The Jukebox Light.*

ROBERT SWARD was born on the Jewish North Side of Chicago. He claims to be a sailor, an amnesiac, a university professor (Cornell, Iowa, Connecticut College), a newspaper editor, a food reviewer, a father of five children, and a husband to four wives. His writing career has been described by critic Virginia Lee as a "long and winding road." In addition to poetry and fiction, he is now producing multi-media "collages" for the World Wide Web. He teaches for the University of California Extension in Santa Cruz, and works as an editorial consultant.

We hope you enjoyed this New Brighton Books title. If you would like to receive information about additional New Brighton Books and products, please contact:

P.O. Box 1674 • Aptos, CA 95001-1674

newbrightonbooks.com

To place an order call toll free 800-919-1779